The Water Beckons

A Swimmer's Story

LINDA HEPWORTH

ISBN: 9781796384505

Back cover photo and makeup courtesy of Deborah Hepworth.
Hepworth Farm 200 Year logo on pg. 30 courtesy of Kyle Hepworth.

Photo Credits: Courtesy of Pacific Masters Swimming, cover photo, pgs. 11, 19, 71, 91, 92, 119, 142, 151, 240, 244. Licensed from
Bigstock, pgs. 31, 43, 47, 51, 60, 66, 79. 96, 100, 101, 104, 145,
147, 155, 194, 201, 212, 216, 221, 223, 230, 231, 234. Wikimedia
Commons, Pgs. 35, 72, 227. Courtesy of t-morales.com, pg. 54.

Printed in the United States

A long whistle signals the start of her event. Up on the blocks she goes, slowly coiling downward and crouching to give an extra push off. "Take your mark." She's heard this direction many times, but this time, it's for her. The electronic buzzer signals the dive, sending Linda, Jeri and eight other swimmers splashing into the water. The race is on.

To Diane + Kathy —

Thanks for the kicking tips!

Linda Hepworth

DEDICATION

Mom has always been there for us.
Over the years, she's witnessed the thrill
of victory as well as the agony of defeat.
This book, and my wonderful life,
is dedicated to Mom.

IN MEMORIAM

My sister Jeri lost her husband, Robert Guy Ryder, on February 6, 2014, just prior to the Nationals. He was a wonderfully supportive man, perfectly suited for my sister. I once asked him how he and Jeri got together and he responded, "When she first walked into the room, I knew I was in trouble."

Jeri's haiku for Robert

When my husband died
My swimming friends around me
We swam butterfly

PROLOGUE

Swimming early with my sisters and brother
Telling a story that is like no other
Over the years, seeking adventures together
A joyful life, travails we can weather

As early as she can remember Linda loved being in the water. She found that swimming in the backyard pool allowed her to dream of her own little world, carefree and serene. Floating on her back allowed her to watch cloud formations become recognizable shapes. Underwater she listened to muted sounds known only to that world. She fantasized about being a mermaid, comfortably weaving through the water in her dreamland. Her cousins, sisters and especially her playful brother often brought her out of her reverie to join in with their impromptu competitions. Sometimes it was a question of who could jump farthest off of the diving board, or who could remain underwater the longest.

Racing each other evolved naturally; from one end of the pool to the other and back again, over and over. These friendly contests were the beginning, a pathway that led to the world of competitive swimming that is now so prominent in Linda's life.

In those early days, it seemed that Linda and her siblings never tired of the water. Their mother had to ask repeatedly for them to get out as the sun was getting low, and it was close to dinnertime. Every evening, she had to promise that tomorrow they could swim again, and the water was reluctantly left behind.

Linda remembers looking back over her shoulder at the pool after everyone had climbed out. The water was settling down, resting from an afternoon of tumultuous activity caused by the swimmers. As she watched, the reflection made by the surface of the water displayed itself on the bottom of the pool. At first it showed a confusion of waves, knocking into one another trying to find some stability. After a few minutes when the only movement was a gentle rocking between the walls of the pool, she saw that the patterns resolved into regular geometric forms, dancing along the bottom. Maybe the water was relieved to be alone, slightly disturbed by the breeze in the air, but Linda always thought the water missed her as much as she missed it.

ONE

~~~~~~

In the beginning...

Linda has been a swimmer all of her life. She comes from a large family of swimmers: four siblings and five cousins who lived next door. She learned how to swim in the backyard pool of her aunt and uncle's house. Summer afternoons were spent splashing and playing games with her family. A perfect respite from the hot humid weather, the water was always refreshing and inviting.

Along with her three sisters and brother, Linda started competing when they were young. They attended a 2-hour swim practice every day after school. Most weekends were spent at meets. Swimming meets were family entertainment. With five swimmers in her family, they became locally well-known in the sport, but it was the summer of 1968 that really put the Hepworth name on the competitive swimming map. For that one year, the four sisters were the right ages to make up a perfect 200-yard medley relay: one from each age group, doing their favorite stroke, for 50 yards. Jeri swam the butterfly in the 16 and under division, Linda wouldn't turn 15 until that autumn, so she fell into the 14 and under age group conquering the breaststroke; Tracy at 12, was a champion in the backstroke. Jodie, representing the 10 and under group, brought it all home with the freestyle. They were proud to be their team's winning relay throughout that summer.

The real test came in August when the family won first place at the County Championships. With plenty of heavy competition, the win instilled a lot of pride in the Hepworth clan. Later that year at the awards party, the team presented the family with a plaque imprinted with the date and all their names. Unfortunately, they misspelled Jodie's name, so "Judie" has been an honorary member of the relay ever since. That event was a highlight of Linda's young life. Decades have come and gone since that pivotal swim. Linda continued swimming and competing during her four years of high school and all through her college years and had many successes. But in retrospect, those memories pale in comparison to the thrill of her entire family sharing in the victory.

After college, life intervened. She moved away from the sport. Forty years flew by. But she never forgot the pleasure of her family swimming together, bonding over their love of the water.

TWO

~~~~~~

She's ready for the day to start, anxious to get to the pool.

The alarm clock is ringing earlier than usual with the promise of a new day. It takes a few seconds for Linda to leave the dream world and open her eyes. As her mind starts to focus, she recognizes a familiar sound, the sound of splashing water. There's a drip in her bathroom sink, constant and insistent, counting off the seconds. *I'll have to fix that*, she thinks, but right now it has a purpose. The sound reminds her that today she is returning to the water to compete in the United States Masters Swimming (USMS) Short Course Summer Nationals, held in Clovis, California.

Even though she's been training specifically for this competition, the reality of it hits her, and she's finding it a bit difficult to stay calm enough to eat a small amount of breakfast, keeping one eye on the clock. She takes a deep breath as she thinks about what she's about to do. Pre-meet jitters have always been a part of the routine. The anticipation and anxiety haunting her this morning is very familiar, just like stage fright that some actors never overcome. The morning has started out to be cool and foggy, as is so often the case in the San Francisco Bay Area. She's ready for the sky to clear, for the day to start. She's anxious to get to the pool.

Linda is part of a team that will compete today. She was lucky enough to find a great group of like-minded souls who call themselves the Rolling Hills Mud Sharks. They are affiliated with the Pacific Masters, a division of USMS. The term Masters sounds impressive, but it just denotes swimmers over the age of 18. USMS is an organization for all levels of skill. Many compete, like Linda and her team will be doing today, but the organization is founded upon the basics of giving adults a place to learn to swim, recreate and stay in shape. Swimmers just out of college in their twenties all the way up to people in their 80s and 90s participate. How truly inspiring to see how the water is the one common denominator that leads to camaraderie and perhaps, longevity.

Established in 1970, USMS is now the premier organization in its field hosting many events including open water swims and adult Learn to Swim classes. Competitions like today's National Championship meet are well-planned events accommodating over 2000 swimmers, all attempting to do the best they can against others in their age group. Linda again feels her nerves jitter as she anticipates the day's activities. A teammate once told Linda that she was so nervous be-

4

fore her swimming meet, she didn't have butterflies in her stomach — she had bald eagles. *Calm down*, she says to herself. *I am a swimmer. I am ready. I can do this.*

─────※─────

When Linda arrives at the venue, there is already a large gathering at the tables set up for registration. Plenty of directions are posted and informative signs indicate where to step into line with the other swimmers. All participants must sign a waiver stating that they are healthy enough to compete. She signs the waiver, and starts to write her initials by each event that she will swim. There it is, the 500-yard freestyle, the first event of the day. She sees her name on the list and not just her name, Jeri's name is listed right above hers, in alphabetical order, of course. It was Jeri who first made the suggestion that they swim this race together since they had swum side by side since they were kids, she confidently confirmed, "We can do this." Apparently Jeri has more confidence in Linda than she has in herself.

This will be the first time that Linda is competing in the 500: 20 laps, non-stop. Months ago, only considering this long event inspired her to train extra hard, just in case she decided to attempt it. Although she has swum that length and more, many times during practices and for fun, now the idea of doing it under pressure at a National meet has her feeling uneasy. Since she had already thrown caution to the wind by telling Jeri and practically everyone else that she was going to do it, there was no backing out now. She sighs deeply, part fear and part anticipation.

Once I get through this event, I'll be fine, she tells herself as she scribbles LH in the designated space. Jeri's events are initialed, indicating she's already here. Linda will keep an eye out for her in the crowd, as she continues to initial the other events she will swim today: 200 yards of backstroke, 200 yards of breaststroke and her last event, the 50-yard backstroke. She does these 200-yard events quite regularly and is not intimidated by them, yet acknowledging the difficulty of her schedule she had consciously decided to end on a fairly easy event. The 50 is just two laps, there and back, a far cry from the grueling 500 she faces as her first race. There's that knot in her stomach again…

During the day, she will also join her teammates in a relay, a special one because Jeri will be swimming with her. About eight months before, when planning for the meet, Jeri signed up with Linda's team even though she lives on the other side of the country, so they could swim on the relay together. It may be an obvious thing to state, but a relay requires all four swimmers to be on the same team. Relays are fun because the whole team is involved. Everyone's working together for a common goal again reminding her of her family's victory.

Among the many meet participants, there is not much conversation, only small talk, nervous chatter and a familiar nod or two. It's early morning, the air is chilly and the competition ahead keeps most everyone's thoughts preoccupied. Everyone's goal is to get signed in and get to the water as quickly as possible.

She follows the red arrows and finds her way into the locker room already bustling with women of all ages, shapes and sizes. The mood is friendly, yet solemn; the swimmers are running on instinct. It is the calm before the storm. Some of the participants have already been in the water and are reporting on the conditions; the temperature of the pool, the lane set ups, and other details.

Everything is numbered: the event, the heat and the lane designated to each swimmer. Competitive swimmers must pay attention to these details. They signify when and where each swimmer will swim and help to move the meet along. A big event like this involves so many people, each responsible for being at the right place at the right time. The officials don't delay the meet for anyone's tardiness.

After all the swimmers are signed in confirming who is actually present, the heat and lane designations are prepared. These lists, the heat sheets, provide a complete schedule of all the swimmers in each event, and they'll be posted as the meet moves along.

Right now Linda is concerned only with putting her suit on, and getting in the water to see how it feels. She has not swum in this particular pool before, so she'll need to do some laps. *Are the edges slippery? What are the particular markings for flip turns? What's the distance between the backstroke flags and the wall? What kind of starting blocks are in use?* All these questions will be answered during the warm-up.

The showers are in use as women clean and warm themselves before the festivities. Linda moves through the crowd and finds a somewhat dry area to suit up. She decides on her favorite blue bathing suit for the warm-up. After that she will change into a dry racing suit to avoid waiting for her event cold and wet, losing energy from shivering.

Collecting all her belongings, she emerges onto the pool deck. She is here; she is finally here, the Nationals! The splashing sounds tell her that the warm-up is already in progress. The morning chill still in the air, a mist rises above the surface of the two heated competition pools. Below it, there is an orderly commotion; the water is churning with swimmers.

The meet starts in thirty minutes. Her first priority is to find her teammates and the area where they are set up. The meet began the day before with the extra long events. To Linda, the 500 is a long event, but some of her gutsy teammates have already competed in the 1000-yard freestyle and the mile long 1650 free-style events. In fact, Jeri was one of those gutsy swimmers, already completing her 1000-yard freestyle. Linda didn't know it yet, but Jeri won a medal, with a sixth place finish. Jeri is a long distance swimmer and does these events regularly. She says she likes the longer events because she isn't the fastest, but she's strong and steady and never quits. What a great way to start a meet, earning a medal for her first swim.

Linda's team had claimed an area on the lawn surrounding the pool and pitched a tent that will house them throughout the weekend. Making her way through the team tents, she easily finds what she's looking for: a banner emblazoned with the Mud Sharks logo. A large cartoon shark wearing a toothy grin and sunglasses is hard to miss. Swim bags, folding chairs and supplies already crowd the tent. Linda is not sure which of her teammates will be joining her today. Some stalwart diehards attend each and every meet. This is commendable. Those like Linda with a full work schedule and other responsibilities swim only a few meets throughout the year. She overheard her coach say that there are about forty team members on the roster for the Mud Sharks. A dozen or so  swimmers come to each workout, maybe 25 come to the meets to compete, but Coach Sharlene says she can get 100 to show up for a party!

Linda finds a spot to set her backpack containing her necessities: swimsuits, caps, goggles, three towels, sun-block lotion, and her favorite snacks to sustain her for the long day ahead. She also brought her warm stadium coat with her name embroidered on it, and a few lucky T-shirts. Everything is piled in a heap, alongside some sleeping bags that have been thoughtfully set out for use. Everything gets sorted out as the day progresses.

The tent is empty of swimmers now. They could be in the locker rooms, at the registration desk or already in the water doing their required warm-up exercises. She had better get in there herself, to work out the anxiety that's been accompanying her all morning.

As she walks through the crowd to the pool, she recognizes many faces but searches for one in particular, her sister Jeri. Maybe she's getting her laps in early. They'll find each other eventually. The two sisters only a year apart in age, now with divergent lives, are on the same path today. Sisters first and foremost, they always pick up their conversations where they had left off, even though months may have passed.

This thought brings Linda back to the present, and what she came here to do today. She needs to start her warm-up. Since all the lanes of both pools are already in motion with swimmers, she has to find a lull in the stream, jump in and immediately start to swim in circles, as they say. Up the right side, practice her flip turn, back down the left side all choreographed with everyone else. She likens this to learning how to jump rope when she was a girl. The rope moved rhythmically and she had to time it just right in order to not stop the flow. She jumps in and starts swimming. The water feels cool but not uncomfortable. This is good. A cooler temperature is a recipe for faster swims, usually.

Coach Sharlene has given specific instructions for the pre-competition warm-up. Swim 600 yards, followed by some anaerobic laps with very little breathing. Next, she'll do some drill work. Drills consist of practice exercises in whatever stroke she is swimming that day. And the meet warm-up ends with a few fast, heart-pumping laps. That is the theory. The reality is that Linda just keeps moving, trying to stay out of the way of faster swimmers. The warm-up can be a circus, a free-for-all, with both men and women literally

bumping into each other, apologizing and moving on.

It's getting close to the time of reckoning, and

she's thinking about her fast-approaching event. Her stomach clenches a bit, with the now all too familiar anxiety. She tries to calm down, reminding herself again that she has rehearsed for this and she is ready. Although she keeps repeating this mantra her stomach is not listening.

Keep swimming, she thinks. *Relax and get those muscles ready.* Taking a deep breath, she executes a flip turn and pushes off the wall, concentrating on her breakout, taking that first stroke. Oops, she nearly ran into that fellow as he was coming into his turn! *Excuse me.* He doesn't seem bothered, just acknowledges her and continues on…such is the warm-up.

She sees a line forming at one of the lanes. *Ah, they've opened up the sprinting lane.* During the warm-up, one lane is designated as a one-way sprint lane. A meet official is acting as a starter. He gives the familiar "Take your mark," blows a whistle and each swimmer in turn, dives off the block, sprints one lap and climbs out. Linda joins those already in line to practice diving from the high, intimidating, slippery, slanted starting blocks twice. The first time her goggles were a bit loose and let in some annoying water, but she tightened them and got it right the second time. She'll do that extra tightening again just before she swims her race.

Linda jumps back into the moving rhythm of the circling warm-up lanes to practice more turns. They are important, especially with the 19 flips she will execute in her 20 laps of freestyle, and she needs to calculate the distance for her backstroke turns in her later events. She'll use the colorful backstroke flags strung across the pool on either end, usually at a regulated 15 feet. She turns over onto her back and starts to count once she's under the backstroke flags: one, two, three strokes. Still kicking, she turns on to her front, and flips over. *Good, three strokes is the correct distance from the wall in this pool.*

She hears someone calling her name. Jeri is there on the side of the pool, and points out where the family is seated in the grandstands with the spectators. Their mom is there, with their other two sisters, Tracy and Jodie excitedly waving to her. The old familiarity comes back with her Mom in the stands, reminiscent of the old days. More than 40 years have lapsed since the summer of 1968, yet the close bond forged by competitive swimming still connects the family members.

She beams at her sister and enthusiastically acknowledges the rest of the family. How did Jeri find her in such a crowd? There is something about a swimmer's gait that is recognizable. Linda has spotted many a teammate by their stroke, and her sister just did the same thing. The fact that Linda wears a bright red swimming cap with her team logo in large letters probably also helps.

Linda is starting to feel ready; her rhythm is coming to her. *Perfect timing,* she thinks, as the call for the swimmers to exit the pool comes through loud and clear. Everyone climbs out, dripping wet. Wrapped in towels, they stand with a hand over their hearts for the national anthem. Linda turns towards the American flag and joins in the salute. With pride and anticipation, the meet has begun. It's show time!

Coach Sharlene, clipboard in hand, arrives on the pool deck. Amazingly dedicated, she knows their event is up and is there to watch and time all their laps. She has been coaching more than 30 years and was named Coach of the Year by the USMS organization. The fact that she never misses any of her swimmers' events is only one of the reasons why she richly deserved the acknowledgment. Her guidance and training helped bring Linda here today. Between her sister's confidence and her coach's encouragement, Linda can't lose!

Alongside her coach are some of Linda's teammates who will act as counters. During the race, they will keep track of how many laps she swims. As Linda nears the wall for her flip turns at the far end, her counters will lower a long pole displaying large plastic digits down into the water: Lap 1, 3, 5, etc. With twenty laps, it is remarkably easy to get confused and swim either too few or too many.

In discussing this upcoming swimming meet with a friend, Linda mentioned the 500 freestyle, the 200 backstroke and the 200 breaststroke. Another friend, not familiar with swimming terms, interrupted the conversation with a question, "Who counts when you're swimming 200 backstrokes?" Linda laughed. She explained that the numbers 500 and 200 designate yardage, not the number of strokes. She then made a quick calculation: at 17 strokes per lap, 500 strokes would be over 30 laps of the pool. No thanks! Right now, 20 is plenty.

Sharlene tells Linda to relax, keep her strokes long and swim the race the way she's been training. She's in Heat 3, Lane 1. As a happy surprise, Jeri will be swimming right next to her in Lane 2. The announcer's voice comes over the speaker: "First event of the day, women's 500-freestyle, 20 laps of the pool." Linda sits wearing her warm stadium coat behind the timers on Lane 1, her lane. She has about 8 minutes to watch the heat of swimmers before her and to contemplate what she is about to do. In the next lane, Jeri does not seem to be nervous and is quietly talking to the other competitors and officials.

Linda is not talking to anyone, trying to visualize swimming 20 laps. *I'll be OK. Relax, breathe regularly; swim with confidence.* Jeri sits down next to her and they both watch the first two heats. Linda keeps count as the women come in to make their turns and head out again. With each lap they complete, Linda's turn gets closer. Almost involuntarily, she starts to take some nervous, deep breaths. Jeri hears her and gives her a hug. They are both proud that at 60 years old, their bodies are prepared to swim all those yards as fast as they can.

In the bleachers filled with spectators, coaches and other swimmers, their mother references a copy of the heat sheets in her lap. She is cheering to her two daughters, hoping they finish well. She has no favorite in the race, and the end results are really not important. It is enough for her to see her children now well into middle age, still competing and sharing each others' lives. She is seated with Tracy and Jodie, both award-winning swimmers with their share of medals and ribbons. However, in recent years they have moved onto other activities. Tracy is a graceful dancer, and Jodie can be found out in the ocean in her kayak.

As Linda glances over at Jeri adjusting her goggles preparing for the race, she thinks of Jeri's husband Robert, conspicuous by his absence. He had just passed away three months before. He would have been in the stands cheering his wife on. The siblings all know that the main reason Jeri is swimming today is to have something else to concentrate on; not to forget her loss, but for just a few minutes, to feel that life can still be normal. This friendly competition is familiar and reassuring to her.

Finally, the first 2 heats are over. Linda hears the whistle for the tired swimmers to leave the pool and now it's her turn. All the training and practices have prepared her for just this moment in time. *Keep breathing deeply, Linda.*

As she approaches the starting blocks, she sees that her counters are in position at the far end of her lane with her coach. Waving enthusiastically and calling her name they try to give her confidence, shouting the familiar team cheer, "Go Linda! Go Jeri! Go Mud Sharks!" Linda attempts a smile through her nerves and weakly waves in acknowledgement.

A long whistle signals the start of her event. Up on the blocks she goes, slowly coiling downward and crouching to give an extra push off. "Take your mark." She's heard this direction many times, but this time, it's for her. The electronic buzzer signals the dive, sending Linda, Jeri and eight other swimmers splashing into the water. The race is on.

THREE

500-YARD FREESTYLE, *LAP ONE*

*Now is the time to put into practice the techniques
she so painstakingly learned.*

Swim, Linda, swim; *20 laps of freestyle.* The 500 is a distance event; pacing is the key. Start slowly, establish a tempo: don't let the rush of adrenalin disrupt her timing. She has to have enough energy to last the entire race. Mentally reciting helps calm her: *This is just the beginning; enjoy the water and the race.*

When one thinks of swimming, usually the first thought is of freestyle. It summons the iconic vision of a prone body moving forward along the surface. Although this is the 500-yard freestyle event, there is really no stroke called the freestyle. In the rules of swimming, the word *freestyle* means swimmers are free to choose whatever stroke they want to swim. The stroke Linda and all the other swimmers are doing now is the crawl, also known as the front crawl or the Australian crawl. It is usually the fastest and the preferred stroke in freestyle events. Pictured here is Laureen Welting, Coach of the San Francisco Olympic Club, showing perfect form. That being said, at sanctioned meets it is

not that unusual for a swimmer to swim the butterfly
during a freestyle event. There could be several reasons; sometimes it's because the athlete wants to get an
official time recorded. However, the name of the game
is to finish first using one's best assets, and some can
"fly" through the water faster than they crawl.

In a recent meet, Linda witnessed a number of
times that swimmers substituted different strokes during the freestyle event. Linda has two teammates in
the 85-89 age group who prefer to swim backstroke
for their freestyle events. One teammate who had hurt
her arm the day before, was needed for a relay and
swam "one-arm freestyle." It was a little slower than
her usual pace, but there are extra points for relays,
and the team didn't want to scratch the event.

Linda watched a young man swim 50 meters of
breaststroke (which is usually the slowest stroke)
while all the other swimmers were doing the freestyle,
or crawl. He was not only keeping up with everyone,

he actually went faster than some. Her teammates all commented on the morale-destroying effect that could have on the other swimmers in that heat, "Gee, I got beaten by someone doing breaststroke!"

Linda laughs at the idea of swimming this 500-yard event doing another stroke. Although it would be perfectly legal for her to do the butterfly, she barely finishes 50 yards of fly at practice. Going ten times that length, under pressure no less, well, she finds that thought quite amusing.

She's worked so hard for this. Now is the time to put into practice the techniques she so painstakingly learned. The breathing pattern that works well for Linda is three strokes, breathe twice and repeat. Getting plenty of air, this pattern allows her to breathe on both sides, where she can watch the competition. She remembers a race where she forgot to breathe and she ran completely out of energy, barely finishing. How can one forget to breathe? Well, the adrenalin rush and excitement of beginning a race is sometimes so overwhelming, it overrules any training. Concentrating on the rhythm of her breathing, her body position, and her upcoming flip turns, she watches her sister churning the water in the next lane.

They are a well-matched pair and can sometimes pace each other stroke by stroke. Here they are again, like the early days, swimming side by side. Just last summer she and Jeri swam an impressively synchronous mile and half together in Brant Lake, in the Adirondack State Park in New York. Across the lake and back again was something they have done for many years.

⁂

Normally, Linda isn't an open water swimmer. To her, there are too many unknowns in open bodies of water: entangling grasses and seaweeds, strange fish and dark scary depths. She prefers the confines and clear water of a well-maintained pool like the one she's in now. But Brant Lake is different. It is her lake. The family cabin on the lake has always been a special retreat for the Hepworths where they all swam, went boating, paddled the canoes and learned to water ski. In retrospect, Linda and her family were very fortunate to have places to swim regularly while they were young. Access to a pool at home and a summer cabin with a lake gave her a lifelong appreciation for the water.

When her sister suggested the across-the-lake swim, Linda knew the routine. They enlisted someone to accompany them in a canoe to signal other boaters there are swimmers in the water, and to provide a ride home, if necessary. They had to make sure there were enough life jackets in the boat for everybody, just in case. A Park Ranger cited Jeri once for not having sufficient safety equipment in her canoe. so they learned to be prepared.

Just as they had done almost all their lives, they swam across the lake aiming for the shore next to the brown boathouse, their landmark. All open water swimmers learn to site a landmark, if possible, to keep on course. After a short rest, Linda and Jeri made the return trip aiming for the red boathouse with white trim, their boathouse. It was the only red one on the lake, and it was their defining landmark, completing

the mile and a half. That was last summer. This is today, doing the same thing but in a serious competition. One of the reasons Linda decided to attempt this 500 was because of that swim in Brant Lake. She had the impression that she could keep up with her sister in a distance event.

She can only see Jeri when she turns her head to breathe because Sharlene has taught her to swim looking down with her head low in the water. The sensation is that of swimming downhill. The lower head allows the water to flow over her body, while simultaneously raising her legs, making her position more hydro-dynamic. Older swimmers can then swim faster by improving their technique without expending more energy. Linda is trying to keep her head low, making use of every physical advantage.

Part of that advantage is following the black line, the lane marker that is required in every competition pool as a guide to swim straight and stay in the middle of the lane. Linda has watched many a swimmer not adhere to this rule, going from one side of the lane to the other, effectively swimming almost twice the distance. She's settling into the rhythm of the race, breathing regularly after every third stroke as she watches her arms pull through the water. Stroke, stroke, breathe. The black T marking tells her it's time to make her first flip turn. Deep breath, stroke, stroke, somersault, push off...

FREESTYLE *LAP TWO*

Flip turns may be difficult to master,
but they can make or break a race.

Stroke, stroke, breathe…

The first lap is over. *Only 19 to go*, she thinks. *I can do this!* Happy that she successfully completed her first flip turn of this race, she got a solid foot landing, no water up her nose, and a good push off. Underwater, her sister is visible in the next lane, pushing off the wall, also starting her second lap.

Linda remembers to take two strokes before breathing. Her coach has explained the physics of the flip turn to the team. There is a forward moving wave that precedes the swimmer, hits the wall first, and then ricochets backwards. Linda's coach taught her swimmers not to breathe for two strokes into the turn, and two strokes coming out of the turn to swim through that swell of water efficiently. Fortunately it has never happened to her, but she's heard of swimmers coming off the wall immediately gasping for air, only to get a mouthful of water instead.

Linda learned to do flip turns as a young girl. Her

family kept up with the latest techniques in swimming. The methods she had repeatedly practiced and perfected were state of the art…at the time. Forty years later, there's a new and more efficient method being taught, so she had to relearn her flip turn. It is sometimes hard for an old dog to learn new tricks, and the flip turn can be difficult to master. It was fortunate she learned the basics when she was young.

The old way was to lower your head, flip your body over and throw your legs into the air. This made a decisive and satisfying splash, but also allowed an unfortunate opportunity to hit your feet, or heels on the edge of the pool if the distance was not properly calculated. Now the coaches teach a flip turn in more of a tuck position, keeping the body curled up, giving an uncoiling-spring effect on the push-off. Because the feet are in so close to the body, there is a lot less danger of heel damage, even though the turn is initiated closer to the wall. It took Linda many a try to learn this new method, but she realized it's a quicker way to turn around.

Flip turns can make or break a race. Linda recalls losing a race many years ago because of a flip turn. She was keeping up with Laurie, a very fast, younger swimmer on her team. The event was the 200-yard freestyle, eight laps of the pool. It was unusual that Linda was keeping up with one of the fastest members of their team. Both were swimming as hard as they could. Everyone was watching, Linda knew, because she could see their coach waving his towel in the air, and hear shouts of encouragement from all the spectators.

When she turned her head to breathe, she could see Laurie's arms moving quickly, right next to hers. Now they were going into the last flip turn of the event. Linda was exhausted and regrettably did a slow, open turn. To this day, she does not know why she made such an amateur move. Her justification at the time was that she felt tired and really needed the extra breath of air.

An open turn involves swimming to the edge of the pool, stopping to hang on, bringing the legs up and then pushing off. This is a four-step process. In contrast, the flip turn, when done properly, does not stop any forward propulsion. The swimmer nears the wall, somersaults, maintaining her momentum in a half circle, and continues in the other direction.

While Linda was "resting" for that split second on the wall, her adversary Laurie flipped, pushed off, and was already a few strokes ahead. The crowd groaned, and went silent. The anticipation was gone, just like that. It was as if the thrill of the intense competition had been suddenly stolen from them. Linda limped home, clearly in second place. She learned a major lesson that day. She had quit, sort of, and vowed to never give up again, especially in competitions.

It's amazing that she can remember a mistake from so far back in her past, like it was yesterday. She appreciates that the memory will definitely prevent her from doing any slow open turns in this competition because she wants to keep up with her sister. Even on the best days, Jeri has better, faster turns, while Linda plays catch up on the straightaway.

Linda continues to work on her flip turns but recently missed one at a meet. She started her somersault too far out and her feet barely touched the wall, giving her no push-off. At least she touched the wall, which made it legal. Not touching would cause disqualification. This particular error wasn't the end of the world; she set a good time in that event. She mentioned the error to her coach with the explanation that she'd been missing them over and over again at practice, so that is what her body is used to doing. The adage that practice makes perfect only works when you practice it correctly!

She makes a mental note to work even more on her turns at practice, but right now, as Linda nears the wall and the familiar black T, she'll just concentrate on this one. Deep breath, stroke, stroke, somersault, push-off…

FREESTYLE *LAP THREE*

Whether she's in the pool, playing in a stream,
or just watching the rain, Linda's dreaming.

Stroke, stroke, breathe…

Jeri is already a stroke ahead as they start this next lap. Linda is still developing her rhythm, conserving energy for the long haul. As she swims along in her quiet world of water, her mind starts to drift back through her memories. She thinks of the family farm where she grew up, and her aunt and uncle's pool where parties were held with her grade school classmates also enjoying the water.

One incident was quite memorable. It was someone's birthday, probably Jeri as she was born in the summer. Many young children were frolicking in the pool when a commotion arose. During a game of "Follow the Leader" one of the young party guests jumped off the diving board following everyone else. She had neglected to mention to anyone that she could not swim. The supervising adults dove into the pool right away to save the struggling girl. She was pulled to safety, and while everything was calming down, there was another unanticipated splash. The almost drowning victim's twin sister repeated the act, jumping off the diving board, also not being able to swim! After another successful rescue, the pool party abruptly ended.

Needless to say, the fact that the two twin sisters, both non-swimmers, followed each other into danger like that stayed with Linda and cemented into her brain the power of family, and especially sister connections. Another lesson she learned that day was that swimming did not come naturally to everyone. Apparently there are those who do not love just being in the water. For young Linda, any chance to jump in with her brother and sisters was always welcome. Part of that may have been because the fun of swimming came only after the farm and household chores were finished.

Every farmer knows about the daily tasks that are required to keep the business going. For several generations her family sold apples and pears in the fall, and peaches, cherries, other seasonal fruits along with sweet corn in the summer. The produce was sold at a roadside stand along with homemade jams, and freshly pressed cider in season. Everyone helped out at the stand; nobody escaped the regimen of the daily farm work, including the grandkids. Grandpa said that all the apples were to be picked and collected, and that included the "drops." Those were the ones that fell to the ground, but were still fresh and good. Four or five young children working for a few hours can laugh, play, throw a few apples and still manage to collect numerous bushels of "drops." Those apples were washed and pressed into cider.

Linda's younger cousins were given different chores suitable to their ages, but they wanted to be like the big kids and get involved with every facet of farming. How Cousin Amy got the keys to the family tractor was never made clear. She sure made an impression on the place, this young girl barely able to reach the pedals, making the rounds on the tractor. She must have taught herself well because today Amy and her twin sister Gail run Hepworth Farms, skillfully maneuvering the trucks, tractors and forklifts. With 500 acres of sustainably grown organic, heirloom tomatoes and other vegetables, their partnership is another illustration of strong sister connections.

Back then, obviously, the kids were not supposed to be on the tractors, but there were other fun machines to use. As she got older, Linda was given the job of assembling the cardboard boxes for the fruits, using the foot-operated stapling machine. Her Dad told her that the machine could be very dangerous. He showed her how it worked and then trusted her to run it safely. The finished package looked sharp: an 8"x 4" box, with a properly stapled handle, proudly bearing her family's logo. She considered it a thing of beauty.

Her least favorite summer chore was picking the currants. Linda found the job of picking the delicate berries off the low bushes very tedious and backbreaking. Young then, with plenty of flexibility in her back and legs, in retrospect, there was nothing to complain about. As a benefit of all the hard work, she was

allowed to eat as many currants as she wanted, but if she ate a lot, there wouldn't be as many baskets filled at the end of the day. Grandpa paid her by the basket, a penny for each one, so quantity was everything. For Linda, it just seemed too hot and dry to spend the whole afternoon working in the dusty fields.

So whenever she could sneak away from the chores, she escaped to a part of the farm where a small stream flowed. It meandered slowly on its way to the

Hudson River, a source of enticement for the kids growing up. Even though her grandmother told of a time when it was clean enough for swimming, by the time Linda was born the river was far too polluted to even consider such a thing. Forbidden to play near the Hudson, she was usually content to be alongside her stream. The constant movement of the water mesmerized her. She rearranged the stones to make small dams just to watch the water overflow and continue on its way.

Throughout the summers, she dreamt about creating her own little world, her water world, using rocks to make up the different towns on the banks. She had barges and boats made from leaves traversing along the way, including imaginary travelers who made the various stops. The constant sound of rushing water let her mind wander. It's the same sound she hears now, the water surrounding her, that's bringing up these memories.

Despite their grandmother's admonitions, Linda and her cousins occasionally escaped to the river. They played on the shore but still got wet, of course, which was considered dangerous. Besides the pollution, the *No Swimming* rules were set because the ebb and flow of the estuarial waters could be deceptively strong for young inexperienced swimmers. To add to the danger, there were train tracks running along the riverside carrying many fast-moving commuter and freight trains to and from New York City. The trick was to avoid the trains and not come home too muddy, so that nobody would guess where they had played all day.

One winter day, two of her cousins, Amy and Charlie, were playing on the ice that had stacked up near the edges of the river. Suddenly a loud cracking sound split the air as the ice the kids were on broke off from the shore and started drifting south. Linda's fast-thinking cousin Amy quickly jumped back to the shore, ran for help and got her brother rescued. That day, the whole town knew where the mischievous Hepworths had been playing.

Linda sees that the wall is again approaching, bringing her back to the present and she initiates another flip turn. Deep breath, stroke, stroke, somersault, push off...

FREESTYLE *LAP FOUR*

Linda always followed her older sister, trying to keep up.

Stroke, stroke, breathe…

She's so happy to be in the water. It's reassuring to know that all she has to do right now is swim these laps, and try to keep up with Jeri. With that in mind, she can't help but think back to when they were kids, growing up on the farm. Linda always followed her older sister around, trying to keep up. They did everything together.

Their aunt, uncle and cousins were next door. Grandmother and Grandfather lived across the road. Completing the grouping, Nannie, her father's grandmother, lived on the other side in the original house on the property. She and Great-Grandpa had inherited the farm way back in the 1800s. Her house was an old style, three-story farmhouse with a large, well-tended garden and two cats. She always said that cats were good on the farm, to keep rodents from taking up residence. There was no pool there, but Nannie's house was a peaceful refuge of a different sort, a place for the kids to spend time and escape their chores.

Surrounding the homes and storage buildings were acres and acres of apple trees with some cherry, plum and peach trees on different lots. One particularly big apple tree, just behind their home held the kids' hide-away tree house. Dad built the roofless platform balanced between three large branches. It had a rope ladder that was not easy to climb, and to add to the precarious aspect of the whole design, the platform was enclosed only by a rope lattice weave.

The kids loved that tree house and spent many an hour up in the tree reading comic books, eating sandwiches and bombarding their cousins with the apples they could easily pick from their high perch. Linda

recalled the time when her brother fell out of the tree house during a sleep-out. The fall was about a ten-foot drop, but he wasn't injured. He had brought all the sleeping bags down with him, and landed safely on the cushioning.

Their house was built atop a hill, providing excellent sledding in the winter. On warm summer days the kids used cardboard boxes to slide, then roll down the hill, straight into the line of cherry trees planted below. They stopped to eat as many cherries as they could, and then climbed back up the hill to start all over again. It was decidedly dangerous for the kids to have been doing that even then. They got rolling rather fast, which was the fun part, but not to Grandma who was responsible for them during the day. "Don't get hurt rolling into those trees" she'd say, as she bandaged numerous cuts and scratches. Linda's Mom recently told her that there would be no more rolling down the hills, since Lyme disease is far too prevalent these days.

Every evening when the chores were done, after the kids were through playing in the mud along the river, climbing the trees and rolling down the hill, it was time to clean up. Linda looked forward to the nightly baths. For her, it was just more play time in the water. It may be dangerous for her to be reminiscing about baths right now, because they conjure up an image of relaxation and she's supposed to keep her mind on racing, but she can't help herself. The memory of the famous bath with her sister Tracy when Linda was about 7 years old still amuses her. She would laugh, if she could.

When they decided to take their bubble bath, the

two young girls thought that this particular occasion called for the entire bottle of bath soap, which made lots and lots of soapy fun. It was even more fun to use all the extra foam to start "washing" the walls of the bathroom. They first started using the washcloths, but soon dropped those in favor of only their hands. This resulted in more creative patterns of soap on the walls.

This was not a bath for relaxation and meditation; they became entranced. The effort to cover all the walls was rather strenuous. The sisters thought their work called out for accompaniment, referring to the concept of "whistle while you work" they had learned from Disney films. They began loudly singing their version of "I Dream of Jeannie with the Light Brown Hair." Linda doesn't remember who thought of it first, but one of them realized that their backsides would cover more area and started rubbing the walls with their entire backs and bums, keeping their movements in time with the music, such as it was. They dubbed this new form of entertainment "wall dancing" and had a discussion about how cabaret singers could adopt this new technique to sing their sultry songs. Covered in bubbles, scrubbing the walls and singing away, Linda and Tracy were lost in their own little dream world of soap and water. That's when Linda suddenly noticed a looming shadow, and saw Tracy's feet fly through the air.

They didn't hear the door open nor see their Dad

come into the bathroom to see what was causing all the noise. He was not happy about the artwork that he called a mess, and reacted by picking Tracy up and getting a towel around her, attempting to clean off some of the extra suds. There were a few stern words and necessary cleaning that took some time, but ever since then, Tracy and Linda have had an affinity for bubble baths and their song. Again, this was just more family bonding in the water.

Looking back, life on the farm was not all work and no play. Linda wonders what Jeri's thinking about right now. Another lap finished as the familiar T bar signals the end of the lane. She's completed four laps, the first 100, one fifth of the way. So far, so good.

Deep breath, stroke, stroke, somersault, pushoff…

FREESTYLE *LAP FIVE*

Her goggles fit so closely, she can feel the batting of her eyelashes.

Stroke, stroke, breathe…

That was a good solid flip turn. Under water she sees her sister slightly ahead of her. *Uh, oh.* With that push-off, some water leaked inside Linda's goggles, thankfully only a small drop. A little bit of water isn't going to be a problem, but it brings to mind how important her goggles are for this distance swim. Goggles can be an issue for many swimmers. Linda used to be worried about them, that they would not stay put during the initial dive off the blocks, that they would be uncomfortably tight or not tight enough, allowing water in. Thankfully, it appears that she will not be plagued by goggle problems in this particular race.

When Linda was a young swimmer, she did not wear goggles during practices or at swim meets. On the way home from the pool she saw rainbows from the streetlights and headlights. It was due to the chlorine-infused membranes of her eyes. Beautiful as the rainbows could be, that exposure was probably not the safest option for her long-term eye health. When she resumed her swimming as an adult, she asked her brother if she had to wear goggles. "Of course you do," Mark told her. "Don't worry about it. You get used to them."

But for Linda it was not easy. At first, they did not fit right and came off on each dive. Worse yet, they once slid down her face, partially blocking her mouth during a race. It's happened to the best of us, she was assured. She's watched many a race where the goggles have slipped and the swimmers just keep plugging through as best they can without getting disqualified. It's usually the first thing mentioned at the end of the swim. "My goggles...!" As heartbreaking as it seems at the moment, a good swimmer just lets it go.

She started wearing goggles at practice but noticed that they came off when she dove in from the starting blocks. So concerned about the goggle situation, she opted to swim without them at the first meet she attended as an adult. Her thinking was that it was better to swim almost blind, than to be distracted by errant goggles. She was really fortunate. That particular competition pool was filled with bromine-salted water, remarkably easy on her eyes. She had no problem seeing the outline of her lane while swimming and there was no discomfort afterwards. Alas, no rainbows.

When Jeri's not sure if her goggles will behave and stay put, she avoids the dive by starting in the water. At the sound of the starting buzzer, she pushes off the wall, perfectly legal in Masters swimming. Some folks are not confident in climbing up onto the slanted blocks, or may have issues with their back or neck that prevent them from diving. Jeri reasons that it may set her back a few seconds at first, but she is a long distance swimmer. When she is swimming a mile (66 laps) or even a 1000-yard race (40 laps), it is much more important to her to know that her goggles are securely affixed for the duration. She must be feeling confident today because she dove in along with Linda and the eight others in this race.

Linda finally found two pairs of goggles that suited her. It took a few races, and many brand names to find the right fit. One is a darkened set for the backstroke, swum face up, providing more sun glare protection. Just like sunglasses, they help her know where she is in her lane. Her other goggles are clear and fit so closely to her eyes she can feel the batting of her eyelashes. She uses these when she dives off the blocks and has them on today. She tightened the straps as much as possible just before she dove in.

Notice the swimmers in big competitions. As soon as their race is finished, they pull their goggles off. The uncomfortable pressure may not be felt while swimming but becomes annoying as soon as the race is over. The tightened goggles also leave reddened depressions around the eyes that take a while to go away. "Goggle eyes" are not always attractive, but swimmers consider them a badge of honor.

Linda feels her shoulders tensing up. Her deltoid muscles have been doing most of the work of pulling her through the water and they're protesting a bit. *Relax*, she tells herself, *and swim.* She remembers to incorporate her core strength, taking some of the tension out of her shoulders. She's been lucky so far today, feeling only a small amount of shoulder tension. She didn't know how her body would react to this race.

When Linda started swimming competitively after such a long lapse of time, she avoided any events longer than 50 yards. She could dive in and speed along for two laps, but after that, she was really winded and out of energy. Fearing that she didn't have the stamina, she was afraid to attempt any longer swims under pressure. Because of her training, she now knows that there is a definite strategy to race swimming, different paces for sprints versus long distance. Start steady, get a feel for the race, build speed, and hopefully finish with a sprint. Very few swimmers can just dive in and sprint the whole race, especially with advancing age.

Her most recent 100-yard freestyle race was a good example of this. She dove in, and the thought came to her. *Follow coach's advice*. She steadied her rhythm, established her breathing pattern, relaxed and what do you know. It was true what Sharlene had told her! She finished still feeling strong and posted a very good time. She got out of the water and yelled for anyone to hear, "I now know how to swim this race!

And here she is today, having come so far, to not only attempt, but to conquer this even longer distance of 500 yards. She wonders how she looks. Did anybody notice her slight change of pace when her shoulder started to complain? Here it is again, another wall, another flip turn. The plastic number tells her she's completed 5 laps already, one quarter of the race. Good thing there are these numbers here. With all this daydreaming, Linda could very well lose count. Deep breath, stroke, stroke, somersault, push off...

FREESTYLE *LAP SIX*

Leaving the farm...

Stroke, stroke, breathe...

Steady swimming, arms pulling, feet kicking, she's getting into the rhythm of this next lap. Her mind continues to drift, recalling days and events from long past, when the steady rhythm of her young life was interrupted by circumstances beyond her control. Her world drastically changed when her family left the farm. In 1965, Linda's dad wanted to break out on his own, chart his own way. Leaving the rural world of agriculture behind to become a salesman, his new job required the family to relocate to Orlando, Florida. The idea of packing up, leaving her playful cousins behind, starting all over in a different state, in a new school was all very intimidating.

Keeping the family's love of water in mind, their dad gave the kids a choice when they were house hunting in Orlando. They could have either a pool in the backyard that would need upkeep, or a house on a lake. The kids heard the word upkeep and naturally thought of even more chores, so unanimously opted for a lake. With over 1500 lakes in Orlando, Florida, there were many choices. The family bought a house overlooking the middle lake of a three-lake chain, named Lake Fairview.

After a day of looking for a runaway family cat that noticed all the commotion and was apparently reluctant to move, the Hepworth family drove from New York to Florida. They made a vacation of the trip by stopping at roadside attractions along the way. One cat named Cleo decided that she wanted to go and rode along in the car with them, but the kitty named Frosty stayed behind and made herself at home with Great-grandma. Cats decide where, and with whom, they want to live.

Despite the fun trip, Linda, just like Frosty, feared the change in lifestyle. She got more and more nervous as they approached their destination. Looking back, her fear was silly and unnecessary. The new reality was nothing to be afraid of. Her family was with her, and their home turned out to be beautiful with an expansive lawn on a serene lake. The best part of the new house was the large, sunken bathtub in her parents' bedroom. There were two steps down, so it was the first "hot tub" Linda ever saw, way before they became trendy. She and her sisters loved taking baths in this tub, as they all could fit in it together, acknowledging the warning to not have any repeat of the sudsy "wall dancing" scenario.

She thinks about those leisurely days with her sisters as she watches her arms churn through the water. She's doing her own form of dancing in a way right now by moving her body in a practiced form, rhythmically swim-dancing. But she has to remember that she's not wall dancing, or in a ballet; she's in a race. Grandma told her many years before that she swam with a nice, pretty stroke but didn't seem to move very fast. In fact, she told Linda that she wanted to get in there and push her along! Maybe Linda was daydreaming through that race too, just like she's doing today. There was another reason Linda did not want to move away from the farm; it meant giving up the close relationship that she had with her grandmother.

Despite all her worries, Linda got settled comfortably in the new environment. There were places to discover, people to meet, and lots of things to do. When the family first arrived at the Florida lake house, the waterfront was completely overgrown by very tall reeds. Dad got all the kids to help and they pulled and tugged those reeds until they had a clearing. This was technically a very large chore, but everybody chipping in made the work easier and fun.

The water was warm and clear, but soon got very muddy as the reeds were pulled out one by one and piled on the yard for disposal. The kids laughed, threw mud on each other, and talked about all the creatures living in this strange lake that were being uprooted by the family's activities of creating a beach. Naturally the lake is home to many aquatic animals including water moccasins, small poisonous snakes that emerge at dusk, but with all the commotion and the churning of the water, the snakes were long gone.

A small wooden dock was built as a diving platform, and the family again had a place to swim.

Oh yeah, swimming. Keep your mind in the present, Linda. Swimming this race is what she's supposed to be thinking about now, her first event of the day. *Pay attention*, she said to herself. Her sister is moving farther ahead of her.

Deep breath, stroke, stroke, somersault, pushoff...

FREESTYLE *LAP SEVEN*

Near-nakedness is definitely a large part of this sport.

Stroke, stroke, breathe...

As Linda streaks through the water in her form-fitting racing suit, she thinks about all the other swimmers participating today and all the different patterns of swim wear Linda saw this morning. The fact that everyone at the meet is dressed only in skimpy bathing suits is taken in stride. Near-nakedness is definitely a large part of this sport. She now accepts this, but as a young girl she was very self-conscious. In her early teen years, donning a bathing suit and emerging onto the pool deck was difficult for her. Swimming every day with a co-ed team changed that.

She remembers a cartoon she saw in a magazine many years ago. The first picture showed a woman going into a dressing room on the beach. As she changed her clothes a man opened the door, mistakenly thinking the room empty. The woman, dressed only in her panties and bra, screamed and tried to cover up. The last picture of the cartoon shows the woman emerging from the dressing room wearing a very small bikini, showing much more skin than when she was wearing her underwear.

That cartoon put it into perspective for Linda. Being caught by surprise in your underwear is not always fun and usually embarrassing. Bathing suits however, no matter how skimpy, can be perfectly proper. An old popular song comes to mind, "It was an itsy-bitsy, teeny-weenie, yellow polka-dot bikini..." Thankfully, Linda's suit is not going to be an issue today. In fact, she's barely thinking about it, which is good. She doesn't need any chafing, bunching or other distractions.

There have been times when the suit itself was the distraction. A few months ago Linda put on a favorite swimming suit. She had worn it more than a few times and it had lost some of its elasticity, but she thought she could get away with wearing it a few more times. After all, it was only for practice. That particular day however, the coach informed the team that they were going to practice starts and turns. Getting ready for a meet meant diving into the water from the starting blocks, instead of just pushing off the wall.

On the first dive, her loose suit was immediately pushed down by the forward impact. She knew right away what had happened but being a pro, she continued swimming along naked from the waist up, with the bunched fabric of the bathing suit producing a terrible drag in the water. She finished her one lap sprint and quickly covered up, hoping that nobody had noticed. But that was not the case! One observant teammate mentioned out loud that she would have gotten extra points at a meet with a wardrobe malfunction like that. Linda retired that particular suit.

Another time, fortunately also at a practice, she was swimming as hard as she could, sprinting. When finished, she stood up, breathing hard and chest heaving. She saw that the coach was giving her a quizzical look, cocking her head and moving her eyes in a sideways direction. What was Sharlene trying to tell her? She then got a bit more assertive with her gestures, trying to be discreet in letting Linda know that one of her breasts had gotten loose, so to speak, and was outside of her suit. Linda didn't feel it, being so intent on her racing and her recovery. It took a while to understand the coach's exaggerated motions and by that time all her teammates saw what had happened. *Oh well, thankfully we're all adults,* Linda thought. She never before thought of herself as buxom, but maybe she should reconsider as now the whole team knows that her breasts apparently don't like to be confined and pop out once in a while to see what's going on.

Early on when she was still in high school, new patterns for racing suits were just coming onto the market. They were a sleek, narrow cut with a lower back. Linda tried one on in the store and realized right away that she would not be wearing this newest fashion. The top part of the suit was very tight and form fitting but not wide enough for her. Her breasts took on a life of their own by peeking out, one to each side. Even then, it was comical. It reminded her of a parody of the song "Tiny Bubbles" sung by the Hawaiian singer Don Ho: "Tiny boobies, on her chest, one looks east and one looks west…" *No giggling in competition, Linda!*

As a kid, Linda enjoyed skinny-dipping. The lake in Florida was her family's watery playground during the day and on warm nights, with the moonlight dancing over the ripples, the lake beckoned. Nakedness gave her extra freedom to appreciate the evening swim. It felt a little naughty because it was so sensual. She loved the water, always felt comfortable in the water.

When the time was right, she and her sisters took off their clothes, and ran quickly from the house to jump into the lake. They tried to be secretive, but the thrill of breaking the rules and running naked in the dark was just too much fun. Instead of whispering their intent, they made a lot of noise, laughing and tripping over the grass to get into the water before they were caught. It was exciting because it was prohibited, and Linda soon found out why.

One particular night the family was splashing

around, not being very discreet. One of her sisters got out of the water to retrieve a towel when she noticed a pair of shoes sticking out from under the hedges lining their property. The polished leather was shining brightly in the moonlight. Douglas, who lived next door, had apparently crouched into the bushes and was spying on the family. He was a young man and there were four naked girls swimming in his back yard. Could anyone blame him?

Loud screams of fright and righteous indignation emanated from the sisters who grabbed their towels and went running back into the house, as upset as the cartoon woman in that beach dressing room.

The happy memory fades as the wall approaches. Deep breath, stroke, stroke, somersault, push off...

FREESTYLE *LAP EIGHT*

Her mind seems to restore itself as she reminisces.

Stroke, stroke, breathe…

This regular pattern of kicking and stroking allows her mind to ramble while her body does the work of pulling her through the water. That's why the sport can be so relaxing, even though it is physically demanding. Her mind seems to restore itself as she reminisces, but she worries that maybe she's doing too much daydreaming. Where is her sister? Linda sees that Jeri is now a few yards ahead.

While Linda is doing all these mental walks down Memory Lane, she wonders what other swimmers think about. In a recent issue of *Streamlines*, the monthly newsletter of the USMS, a champion swimmer, Terry "Speed" Heggy wrote about the concept of mindful swimming. Concentrating on technique is good, but it's OK to let the mind wander, he wrote, "Swimming is a big part of our lives, but it's not the only thing we think about. Thoughts about family, work and what's for dinner can float through our heads as we float through the water. This isn't necessarily a bad thing; swimming is a great way to relieve stress and relax, even while we're working hard. Singing, thinking about to-do lists, and anticipating an upcoming vacation are all legitimate things to do as we crank out laps to get a good cardio workout."

1952 Helsinki Olympian Gail Roper does not follow that advice. She describes how her focus is completely on her stroke. She sets her body position, anticipates the angle of entry for her arms, and knows

when she executes the "catch"—feeling the water being moved behind her as she presses forward. Gail is considered a pioneer in the sport, blazing trails by studying everything she could find about increasing speed in the water. When asked why she is a champion, Gail responded, "Determination."

One of Linda's friends mentioned that she finds it rather boring to do lap swimming, just going back and forth, and asked how Linda occupies her mind while swimming 3,000 yards each workout. Linda told her that Coach is very helpful in keeping her mind busy. She divides the workout into sets, giving the swimmers different concepts to work on while they do their yardage, all the while helping to keep them mindful. She also directs her swimmers to concentrate on a particular body position, a breathing technique, or building the kick. With each instruction, Linda has something to think about, and the laps fly by.

And personally, Linda can add math lessons to her thoughts. When she isn't reminiscing to herself, she counts her strokes and her laps, constantly adding and subtracting. How many she has done? How many to go? Numerical concepts keep Linda's mind busy as she divides this swim into repeating 100s. To her way of thinking, somehow doing five repetitions, which she does at practice all the time, seems less of a daunting task than the idea of swimming 20 laps nonstop. She thinks about how swimming has helped her with proportion and division. However she still finds the clock, with its sixty-second base, challenging.

Coaches are big on interval training, having their swimmers swim repeated laps on set timed segments to maintain a certain pace. The easy one is to go "from the top" on the one minute. Most of the swimmers can handle that one because no calculation is required; the swimmers leave the wall when the clock hits twelve. But then Coach gets creative, telling them to go every fifty seconds, or one minute-ten seconds, or even harder to compute is the one minute-forty second interval. Linda often goes off before, and sometimes after the other swimmers, being easily confused by the divisions of sixty seconds. And to think she's supposedly good at math! She once told Coach Sharlene that apparently she could not swim and calculate at the same time.

Her friends asked her what the difference was between swimming in a 25-yard pool (like the one she is in today) and swimming Long Course, in an Olympic sized 50-meter pool. Linda had the answer. It takes her about 17 strokes of freestyle to get to the end of a 25 yard pool but 44 strokes to go one length of 50 meters. The difference is twice the length plus 10%. The fact that she had those numbers available in her head surprised everyone. When she counts in practice, her laps seem easier. If she's not careful she'll be envisioning herself in a classroom, not a swimming pool.

Concentrate on this race, Linda. Deep breath, stroke, stroke, somersault, push off…

Linda may have been kidding herself
that she could keep up with Jeri.

Stroke, stroke, breathe…

Jeri is far ahead now. Linda consciously decided to not speed up to catch her; it's too early in the race. Her pacing is more important. She needs to finish strongly. Sharlene has told Linda many times to swim her own race. "Don't be distracted by the other swimmers." Linda thinks back to another race when she did not heed that advice because of a swimmer she knew from her youth, Judy. Judy kept up with the sport as an adult and reconnected with Linda at one of the recent California meets. Judy was also a member of the 1968 team, present when the Hepworths swam their famous family relay. The two friends reminisced about their days of youth, speed and glory.

Linda saw Judy's name on the heat sheets and was delighted to see that her old friend was going to be swimming in the lane right next to hers. They were to swim 200-meter freestyle, in a long course pool. In that venue, a 200 is four lengths of the pool. Linda easily recalls that particular swim.

As the swimmers congregated at their proper lane designations, Linda looked over at the next lane expecting to see her old friend, and saw a stranger instead. *Where's Judy?* Linda thought this must be a joke. There was someone in "Judy's" lane, but it was not her friend. It was a stranger, yet she was wearing the same team suit and cap Linda had seen on Judy. This was very confusing. It only made sense later, after the race, when she discovered that there are two Judys on that team, coincidentally with the same last name. Meanwhile Linda was supposed to be preparing her mind for the imminent contest, but was distracted by the dilemma of this different, unfamiliar Judy. Linda stepped up onto the blocks with the puzzling question still in mind. She wasn't concentrating on her race.

The starting whistle blew. She dove in and immediately started to swim hard and fast to impress this new Judy. This was a distance event, four laps of a long course pool and needs a strategy. Linda did not have this in mind, did not pace herself, and soon ran completely out of energy. She was giving herself excuses: *I'm not used to swimming long course. I didn't warm up enough,* and *I didn't sleep very well last night.* Negative thoughts permeated her mind; the end of the pool looked really far away. With each stroke, her arms felt like lead.

She got so tired that she actually considered stopping and climbing out after only three laps, but that wasn't an option. It would be quitting, and she's not a quitter. She managed to complete her third flip turn, lowered her head as coach had instructed and slowly swam the last, very long lap. She could see Sharlene on the side of the pool encouraging her, knowing what had happened; she had seen that pained loping stroke before when fatigue had set in after a grueling practice. Linda had made a beginner's mistake and had "gone out too fast."

Linda finished, but was not happy. Sharlene was sympathetic, "It's OK. Don't worry. It's only the first race of the day for you. Consider it a warm-up." The new Judy was funny, "At first you were right with me, and then I don't know where you went!" Linda's vow that day has stayed with her. *Swim your own race at your own pace, and just keep going.*

At this point, it seems that Linda may have been kidding herself that she could keep up with Jeri in a long race such as this one. They did have that synchronous swim across Brant Lake last summer. Perhaps Jeri was just being nice that day, swimming slowly on purpose to stay close to Linda in the open water. But there was another event several months previously that had added to Linda's feeling of confidence to swim this race against her sister.

Although she and Jeri live across the country from each other, when there's the opportunity, they go to swim practices together. One of those practices unexpectedly turned into a competition. They were visiting their brother Mark in Texas and decided to go to the pool and get in a few laps. Jeri suggested they begin with a slow 500 as a warm-up. She deliberately used the words, "slow" and "warm-up" but that's not how it turned out. Apparently the competitive nature of the two sisters soon took over. Linda doesn't know who started it, but as they were swimming along, they both began picking up speed. Each sister was watching the other closely, trying to stay ahead and they ended up racing, lap after lap. It was so impromptu and such a close race that all the other swimmers noticed, some of whom stopped their own exercising to watch. Twenty laps is a long race to a seasoned swimmer and to the uninitiated spectators, not used to such a spectacle in a community pool, it must have seemed interminable. Are they ever going to stop?

The sisters ended on an outright sprint, Jeri finishing just slightly ahead of Linda. As soon as they

caught their breath and were able, they started laughing. Their competitiveness had taken control and transformed what was to be a casual swim into an event. Apparently it was something to see; a sizable audience had gathered. Linda herself may have wanted to watch such a race if she wasn't the one in it!

It was a mutual decision that they had done enough for the day and their "casual, just for fun" swim practice was over. As a passing thought, Linda wishes she could substitute that race for the one she is in now, but there's no room for regrets when her mind is so full of wonderful memories. Maybe she can get a really good push-off on this next turn and make up some of the slack between her and Jeri. Deep breath, stroke, stroke, somersault, push-off...

FREESTYLE *LAP TEN*

When her family began swimming competitively
in earnest, Linda was a holdout.

Stroke, stroke, breathe…

Linda's coming to the halfway mark now with the number 9 clearly visible for that last turn. The counters are doing their job. Since she's been doing so much daydreaming, she better not trust her own idea of where she is in this race. She thinks that if worse comes to worse, she will just keep swimming until she sees Jeri stop. That's one benefit of being behind.

At a meet a few years ago, Linda was swimming a 200-yard freestyle race in a 25-yard pool, 8 lengths. She had no counters putting plastic numbers down for her to see, so she wasn't sure as she made a flip turn whether she had done 5 laps or 7. *Oh dear,* she thought. *What am I going to do?* The good news at the time was that she was behind the other swimmers. She watched as they came into the next turn, flipped and kept going. The good news was that she now knew she had 2 more to go. The bad news was that she was tired, and still had 2 more to go…

Although it's not the best scenario for her to be behind the other swimmers, it is not unfamiliar territory. When all her family began swimming competitively in earnest, Linda decided against it. At the time, she wasn't interested in working that hard. It seemed too difficult to learn how to swim all the strokes, the dreaded flip turns, the brisk early mornings, etc… She could go on and on about the hardships.

So Linda stayed home while her brother and sisters went off to practice for a few months. Not wanting her to be idle, her Mom offered a suggestion. Why not take art lessons? An artist friend of the family volunteered to tutor Linda. This was perfect. She had some talent for drawing, and learning techniques from a pro seemed a great way to pass the summer.

Linda loved the art lessons. Her teacher was a very private man who lived in a small tidy house. He did not ordinarily give lessons but opened up his studio to Linda as a favor to her parents. She listened well and was proud of the drawings she took home every week. At first she learned to draw what is referred to as still life: bottles, glassware and fruit. Emphasis was put on light and shading. These two concepts work together to artistically convey a curved surface on a flat piece of paper. She was collecting many drawings of bottles, each one getting more realistic.

As the summer progressed, she moved onto drawing trees. Her art teacher explained about natural shapes. She was told to make her branches reach up in positions seen in the wild. Without it being said, Linda was learning about the universal mathematical pattern that is common throughout nature. Adhering to this idea gave her drawings realism and has helped her understand what defines beauty in this world. The summer of art lessons was a study in thoughtfulness.

While she was quietly drawing, the rest of her family was involved with the rush and excitement of athletics, training with their swimming team. She sometimes went to the pool and watched the practices as they learned to swim faster, using streamlining techniques that efficiently moved them through the water. The lessons in art and observations about swimming were connected: moving through the water can be likened to a tree spreading its branches upward. Both describe a reaching motion that is dictated by the physical world around us.

After the summer art classes were finished, Linda decided that she wanted to learn to swim like a pro. She began to join them with the regular routine of swim practice. Because she was a few months behind, Linda had to "catch up" to the rest of the family.

And here she is again, a bit behind, trying to "catch up" to her sister. She's finished 10 laps, the halfway mark.

Deep breath, stroke, stroke, somersault, push-off...

FREESTYLE *LAP ELEVEN*

Swimming like Esther Williams is not good for racing.

Stroke, stroke, breathe...

Her brother and sisters helped ease Linda into the routine of swim practices, patiently explaining what the team was doing: techniques, dives and the dreaded flip turns, but it still took her some time to become proficient in the water. She had bad habits to break. One of those was swimming with her head out of the water. Her mother calls it swimming like Esther Williams.

Esther Williams was a champion competitive swimmer who missed out on the 1940 Olympics due to the outbreak of war. She then made a career of swimming in movies. She brought prestige to the sport along with another swimmer, Johnny Weissmuller, famous for his role as Tarzan. A glamorous swimmer, Esther wore a stylish bathing suit and cap, beaming with her trademark smile as she swam.

Apparently Linda still remembers that way of swimming. Sharlene constantly reminds her to keep her head low to maintain a streamlined position. She tells Linda to "Think of my hand on your head pushing it down." Linda was practicing this new technique,

described as swimming downhill, concentrating so hard that she did not pay attention to the fact that her lane was coming to an end and swam smack into the wall, head first. She felt the impact and heard the thud. Apparently everyone else at swim practice heard it too. This is not a smart thing to do. It's embarrassing in front of her teammates, and downright dangerous. Fortunately, her thick cap absorbed most of the force. Sharlene told her that it was a bit special. She had seen others swim into the wall doing backstroke because they miscounted their strokes, but not too many swimmers could brag that they were so lost in thought they literally did not see the wall coming. Afterwards, Sharlene kept asking if she was all right and kept an eye on her. Linda got a small bump on her head from the accident, and thought she had learned a lesson to stay alert. She has no reasonable explanation as to why she did it more than once.

Fortunately, the second time it happened she was swimming a drill of freestyle. These exaggerated movements train the body to be in the right position. This particular drill called for one arm to be stretched out in front of her as she swam on her side. Thankfully her outstretched hand hit the wall first that time, saving her from another possible concussion.

Linda's teammates must like having her at practice; she provides entertainment with breasts popping out and swimming into walls. In addition, Linda is known to tell a joke here and there and two appropriate jokes pop into her mind:

What do a dentist and a swim coach have in common? They both use drills.

Two fish swim into a concrete wall. One turns to the other and says, "Dam!"

Try to keep the jokes to a minimum, Linda says to herself. *It's hard to laugh under water. You're supposed to be competing. This is not the time to be joking around.*

And remembering when she bumped her head, Linda has to add another admonishment to the list; *stay alert and keep your eyes open!* Her sister Jeri is probably not telling herself jokes, and is no doubt paying attention to all the signs that her lane is coming to an end, completely concentrating on her swim. That could be why she's ahead.

Linda again wonders if she should speed up. *Not quite yet,* she decides. *It's too early in the race.* Concerned she will run out of energy, she'll stick to her original plan: keep her present pace for a few more laps then increase her speed, if she feels good, at the 16th lap. That was the original strategy for this race. Speeding up for the last 100 yards may be a way to catch up to Jeri.

Linda notices the backstroke flags come into view, then sees the black T bar and the number 11. She pays attention to these signs. She does not think the spectators need any extra entertainment today so she will not be swimming into any walls. Deep breath, stroke, stroke, somersault, push-off...

FREESTYLE *LAP TWELVE*

The family yearned for even more water adventures.

Stroke, stroke, breathe...

When Linda's family joined the swim team in Orlando, the team was delighted. Their presence added four at first, and then when Linda joined, five new swimmers to the roster. More swimmers meant they could build relays and win extra points at meets. The Hepworths' involvement couldn't have come at a more opportune time for their new affiliation. The team was about to lose their rented place to swim. The old Orlando *Aquaseum* was being closed. It was a rather dilapidated concrete pool and building, expensive to refurbish, plus the city had plans for redevelopment in the area.

The Hepworth home, with its cleared lakefront, became the temporary practice spot for the team. All the swimmers showed up about 4:30 each weekday afternoon. Coach Jackie stood on the little dock and held practice in the lake. This agreement worked well. Linda's Mom did not have to drive the kids anywhere. The only drawback was the family dog Tina.

Beloved Tina was a large drooling St. Bernard who also loved to swim and very much wanted to be included in the festivities. Her name was shortened from her given name of *Ach, du Lieber Augustine,* from an Austrian song title of the 16th century, which translates to "Oh you dear Augustine." There was a slight mix-up when Linda's father went to register the new pup's name with the AKC. Nobody had told him how to spell it, so he registered her as Augustine Von Hepworth. The new moniker wasn't as classy as the one the family had originally selected, but it would do, and Tina became part of the family.

The dog was a bit perturbed by the commotion of all the team swimmers showing up every day, and took revenge. Tina stole towels, at least one a week. Practice time was over, and sure enough, somebody's towel was missing. Sometimes the swimmers caught Tina stealing and chased her. This did not help. In fact, it encouraged her. Tina would run a bit of a distance away, stand on one end of the towel and rip it. She appeared to enjoy the sound of the tearing fabric. She waited until they almost caught up with her then took off again, each time shredding more of the towel. What fun … for the dog!

Later on, the family found the ripped and shredded towels stored away under a bush in the garden where Tina had hidden them. Linda's not sure if her mother had to replace any of the ruined towels.

Linda thinks about her own towel and where she

left it at the side of the pool during her swim. There are over 2000 swimmers at the pool today, but she knows that her towel, shoes, and the warm stadium coat with her name embroidered on it will still be there waiting for her. There is no fun-loving dog here today to abscond with her possessions.

Recently, someone did bring a Labrador retriever to a swimming meet. At first the dog behaved well just watching all the excitement, but then decided to get into the act. Labs are water dogs and this one decided to jump in during the competition. Fortunately, no one was swimming in the lane that the dog chose, so there was little interruption in the proceedings. Everybody understood the draw of the water, and the Lab was gently escorted off the premises.

The Lab was instinctively drawn to the water. So are ducks. Linda and everybody else couldn't help but notice them when they landed making quite a splash. The announcer laughed and said as long as they didn't bother anybody, they were welcome to be a part of the

competition. There was probably more commotion in the water than they were used to, so they didn't stay.

Her thoughts return to Florida. The lake was fun, swimming and sailing on their Sunfish sailboat, but the family yearned for even more water adventures. For a change of pace they drove to the famous Daytona Beach. Orlando is centrally located in Florida with the Gulf of Mexico about an hour west; heading east to Daytona takes about the same amount of time. Her father had bought the family an early 60s yellow Pontiac Tempest convertible. It had an interesting feature: the new push button transmission, which made the kids believe that this was truly a futuristic car. It was the perfect "go to the beach" car, of course with Tina the dog in the back seat. She paced back and forth, drooling over the excitement of being included in the family outing.

The Hepworths didn't go to the Gulf much, preferring the thrill of driving along the ocean's edge literally, at Daytona. The sands are naturally so firmly packed that cars can drive right on the beach; the "roadway"

runs parallel to the shore dividing the beach into half with beachcombers on one side and surging tides on the other. Linda could see why Daytona was known for its car culture. If one tires of cruising the beach, the famous Daytona Speedway is right down the road for faster action.

Just like those car races, Jeri speeds by in the next lane, going the other direction. She's almost half a lap ahead now, well into her 13th lap.

Deep breath, stroke, stroke, somersault, push-off...

FREESTYLE *LAP THIRTEEN*

Now she was experiencing a rare cap mishap.

Stroke, stroke, breathe ...

In the beginning of this race Linda's adrenalin was pumping, getting her through the first few laps. Now she's settled into her rhythm, following along the black line while keeping her eyes open. Where was she before she was interrupted by another necessary flip turn? Oh yeah, thinking of her childhood in Florida.

Living in Florida provided other watery delights new to Linda. It rains a lot, almost every day. She played outside, even in the rain, as it was usually warm. The kids did not stop their outdoor activities on account of a bit of drizzle in the air. Because of the amount of rainfall, there are deep ditches along the roads to collect the runoff, filled with water, and God knows what else.

This was no concern to Linda at the time as she and her new playmate, Taffy, devised a game. They collected a large pile of oranges that had dropped from the neighbors' trees, donned their bathing suits and climbed into the water-filled ditches along the road. From their hidden positions, they rolled the oranges across the road, one at a time, with the object of getting the orange all the way to the other side, avoiding passing cars. Whenever an orange successfully made it across the road, that was a time for celebration and points were accrued. But if the orange got hit by one of the cars' tires, always associated with a funny squish noise, well, that was hilarious. This was a win/win situation for the pre-teen girls.

Looking back, Linda thinks, *Really? Did I do that? I actually played in drainage ditches?* At this point in time she certainly knows the danger in such an activity. There are water bugs and water snakes in Florida, not to mention whatever grime was draining from the roads. At the time, the water appeared clean, clean enough anyway, that the stupidity of what she was doing did not occur to her. Now she is a bit horrified at the idea. Her parents did not know of this particular game; they would have put a stop to the fun.

Besides the inherent dangers, Linda now thinks of the waste. She grew up with her Grandfather's rules that no fruit or food should ever be wasted, and there she was rolling edible oranges, her neighbor's oranges, across the road to be flattened. It is amazing what kids will do to entertain themselves, and to be honest, Linda still smiles when she thinks of the hours of fun she had with her friend hunkered down in the drainage ditches.

Back to the present, with that last push-off, Linda's swim cap started to move and creep up on her forehead. She was so worried about her goggles giving her trouble, concentrated so much on them, that she hadn't given much thought to her cap. Now she was experiencing a rare cap mishap. The air bubble that's causing the creeping will grow with every somersault. The cap will continue to fill up and slip off if she doesn't grab it somehow and pull it down. She'll have to wait until she begins her next turn, reach up quickly and yank the cap down. Two hands pulling simultaneously would do the trick, but that means she'd have to miss a stroke; break her form, so to speak. One tug on the cap seems the least disruptive way to go. Good thing she's doing the crawl, or freestyle in this race. The breaststroke or butterfly needs to be swum with the arms synchronous at all times. She would be disqualified if she broke her form just to rescue her cap. In that case, she would have to let it fill up, fall off, or do whatever it wanted to do.

She devises a plan. As she nears the upcoming wall, she can use her left hand to push the air out of her cap while her right hand gives it a tug. Hopefully that is all she'll need to pull the errant cap down into its correct position and avert a crisis. She relaxes a bit; she won't actually lose her cap. She's thinking that it can't fall off because her trusty well-behaved goggles act as a strap to secure it, usually. But then she remembers a very unusual cap crisis during a grueling 1500. The 1500 is a long race, 60 laps. Linda's teammate Annette does these distance events and is proficient at them. Right in the beginning of one of these races she felt her cap start to inch up her forehead. It kept moving back with each flip turn. Soon, the cap was covering only the crown of her head. It finally came off on lap number 14.

It was terribly upsetting. Even though Annette had tied her hair up before she put her cap on, when the cap came off, so did the tie. Her hair floated around her as she swam, filling her mouth as she tried to breathe. Flip turns were out of the question. She had to do open turns to gulp air. And she had 46 more laps to go. Although disheartened, she kept at it and finished with a remarkably respectable time. What a trooper.

After her swim, she enlisted an employee at the pool to dive down and retrieve her cap. She couldn't get it herself because she was out of breath for one thing, and the pool was deep: 17 feet deep. The whole team heard about Annette's cap misadventure. An interesting side note — her goggles stayed on even though they were strapped to the outside of her cap. Annette wasn't sure how that trick happened, but was thankful. She couldn't breathe, but at least she could see.

The next morning, Linda and Annette were standing at the edge of the pool, getting ready for the day's events. Linda noticed a cap, another one, at the bottom of the deep pool and pointed it out to Annette. It had been left there all night, abandoned by its owner who probably did not want to use it again, since it fell off. A swimmer loses confidence in equipment that fails,

especially dur-
ing a competition.
Linda now wishes
she had not re-
membered that
particular cap epi-
sode. It makes her
worry. She doesn't
want to add to any

more caps at the bottom of the pool.

She's coming to the wall and gets a brainstorm. Executing her flip turn, the first thing she does is duck her head down. As she somersaults, her hands come up past her ears to get into the streamline position. Maybe she can use those motions to tug on her cap without making too many extraneous motions. She takes a moment, a split second, really. As her hands go past her cap, she grabs the edges and pulls with both hands. Since she is almost upside down, the water bubble rises and leaves her cap. Success! Linda is not sure of Sharlene's reaction to such a maneuver, if she noticed and wonders if anybody noticed. Maybe she'll hear about it later.

Right now she is relieved that her cap is back in position, and she won't relive Annette's nightmare. As all of this is happening, Linda reads the number held by her counters: 13. If she had lost her cap, it would have occurred on fateful lap 14. She'll have to tell Annette.

Deep breath, stroke, stroke, somersault, push off…

Swimmers must practice mindfully to overcome bad habits.

Stroke, stroke, breathe…

Oops. Linda's feet slipped and did not make a strong contact with the wall that time, because she was concentrating on fixing her cap. *Kick harder; try to make up for any lost time. Don't worry about that less than perfect flip*

turn. Even though she did not appreciate them at the time, the chores she was assigned on the farm taught her that no matter what needed to be done, even if she made a few mistakes along the way, it would be all right if she just persevered.

She incorporated that idea into practice one day when a visiting coach told the swimmers ahead of time what the workout was going to be. The day's events included hard repeats, finishing with a timed sprint 100. Normally Sharlene does not tell her swimmers what she has in store for them. She doesn't want them to worry or worse yet, get out of the pool and not complete the practice.

With dread and apprehension, Linda went through her laps with that nagging last 100 foremost in her mind. To Linda, sprints are like chores. They need to be done, but they're not always fun. So when it was time, and the clock hit 12, Linda took off, swimming as fast as she could. Halfway down the pool, she noticed that she was alone. Her teammates were not following, but she had already committed, so she sprinted four laps all by herself. When she finished, breathing hard and looking around questioningly, she found out that the coach had told everyone to take a few minutes and do some slow laps before the last sprint. Linda had been so intent on getting through the unpleasantness, that she had missed that very important bit of instruction.

The ritual of practice — hard, challenging and never boring — is the necessary price to pay for excellence. However, practicing does not mean just going through the motions to get it over with. The idea is to train the body to do things correctly and efficiently, so they become second nature under pressure in a competition such as this one. Like all athletes, Linda should be practicing mindfully to overcome bad habits that hold her back from improving. Sloppy flip turns are an example of this—although that last one can be forgiven.

Mostly at practice, if she does not concentrate fully, she forgets techniques and loses her form. For instance, her arms are strong and sometimes she lets her legs almost drag behind. This is not efficient as she is not getting any propulsion from the rear. All her coaches have told her to use her legs. "Concentrate on a three-beat kick." Three kicks to each arm pull. And sometimes for a harder work-out, Coach instructs the swimmers to use a six-beat kick. When she does it correctly, Linda sees that it increases her speed, making the "chore" of swimming less daunting. The drawback is that using the large leg muscles uses a lot more oxygen, which translates into fatigue. Therefore, in a distance race such as this, Linda does not kick as hard as she would in a shorter, faster, sprinting race.

Linda recently watched swimmers compete in the televised International Paralympics. This is a special meet for folks who have lost limbs or were born with other limitations. One man who had no arms swam the 200-meter backstroke, using a dolphin kick on his back, completing four laps of the 50-meter pool in an astoundingly fast time. After seeing that, Linda went to practice and told everyone that she now knows the importance of the kick.

Olympian Ryan Lochte promotes a style of practice that starts with kicking only, adding the arms later. The trick is to get to the other side of the pool using less arm strokes each lap. The swimmer's legs really do most of the work here. Linda watched an Olympian from China named Sun swim 500 meters in a long course pool, using an astoundingly few arm strokes on each lap. Linda counts about 17 pull strokes for each lap of a 25-yard pool. Sun was using less than that to complete one lap of 50 meters, more than twice the distance. He was winning, too! His legs were the power source. Linda went to practice after that and excitedly told everyone that she wanted to swim like Sun. But right now, she's just swimming like Linda.

Her mind quiets while she concentrates on her legs and counts her three beat kick. Kick, kick, kick. Kick, kick, kick. Three kicks for every arm pull. It takes all her concentration to do this, because she has not made it a habit. The strategy seems to be working, as the familiar black T-bar is now underneath her.

Deep breath, stroke, stroke, somersault, push-off...

FREESTYLE *LAP FIFTEEN*

Off to Westchester County...

Stroke, stroke, breathe...

She continues her journey with the pattern of her kick. 1-2-3, 1-2-3. The repetitious meter lulls her thoughts back to the big changes in her life growing up. Her mind is filled with a passing parade of memories of her life in Florida: a new house, a new school, and new friends. Her world now revolved around the daily routine of swim practice and competitions almost every weekend. Life was changing for her parents as well.

Dad stayed with the sales job for a while, but then branched out into other endeavors. He worked for a few corporations at first, testing the waters before going into business for himself. He bought a packing-house for grapefruit and oranges, and the family found itself again in the world of farming. Linda always joked that the family went from apples to oranges. When the kids got a tour of the new facility, they commented that all the fruit on the conveyor belt looked so shiny; the apples for sale back on the New York farm were never this shiny. Their dad explained, "These fruits are waxed for a prettier appearance on the grocery shelves." The kids were skeptical, not used to the new, improved way of doing things. They were also not convinced the fruit tasted any better, despite the appearance.

With all the water normally associated with Florida, no one expected the drought that began a few years later. There were fewer fruits coming into the packing-house, eventually causing Linda's dad to declare bankruptcy. He soon had another idea and went to work for Merrill Lynch, Pierce, Fenner and Smith, as the huge financial firm was originally called. Not fully understanding the nature of such a big corporation, the kids asked him why the name Hepworth wasn't immediately added to the masthead.

Their dad was now working in the commodities market, betting whether or not the farmers would make any money on any given year, on certain crops, and how much. Because he was first and foremost a farmer himself, he knew the ups and downs of the business and especially weather-caused hardships. He did quite well. His success ultimately led to another move; back to New York. Not back to the farm, but closer to New York City, where all the financial business is conducted. This meant more change and disruption of routine for Linda, who did not take these matters lightly.

So, off to Westchester County the family went. The year was 1968. It became immediately apparent that they had definitely left Florida, and its laid-back ways. The family had been accustomed to their dad going to work dressed in the traditional conservative black suit, white shirt and dark tie. Now that her dad was commuting into New York City to the financial district, he wanted to look sharp. His new attire included large colorful ties and wide lapelled double-breasted suits, very fashionable for the time. He was branching out with the new 1960s fashions. Like everyone else at the time, he wore his hair longer.

Looking back, the change may have been more of a shock to Linda's mother than to the kids. Their dad was hip! He was listening to all the groovy music of the day. Dad was the one bringing home contemporary music records. Iron Butterfly with their iconic album entitled *In a Gadda Da Vida* was the one Linda really liked with their driving beat. Also popular at the time were The Beatles, Crosby, Stills and Nash and Judy Collins, and these could be heard throughout the home.

The family settled into the routine in this new location, including dividing up all the household chores. Linda opted to do the ironing; she found it relaxing. So she did most of the ironing for the family, making sure that her dad had crisp white shirts ready to wear to work along with his ever-expanding assortment of colorful ties. With so many people in the house, sometimes laundry got backed up. It happened one day that Dad did not have a clean white undershirt. Linda found out later that he got strange looks from co-workers as he was forced to wear a red and black horizontally striped T-shirt under his crisply ironed white business shirt. Apparently the bright stripes were visible, and this was something that simply was not done in the conservative atmosphere of the financial district. That one incident gave him a reputation for being somewhat of a rebel.

Instead of the modern house in Florida, this Westchester County home was old, with four floors and six bedrooms. There was a separate bedroom for each kid for the first time in their lives, a place they could call their own and decorate according to their tastes. The house had been built in the 1800s and had lots of charm. Much to everyone's surprise, the basement even had a coal chute from the days when the heating came from a coal furnace and a non-operating, but never-the-less entertaining dumb-waiter! The kids loved this new house.

No swimming place, at first, but there was a stream that ran past the house. The Hepworths moved a lot of rocks, damming up the stream enough to make a swimming hole, just for the summers of course. Their neighbors had a very modern home with a small pool built into the side of the house. It was just outside the kids' bedroom. The kids thought this was terrific, and spent as much time there as they could without being rude. On the other hand, the neighbors thought that the makeshift swimming hole the Hepworths had set up was even better and wanted to swim there. It may be human nature to want what you don't have.

Neither of these two watering holes was set up for racing. They were for cooling off, quick dips in the afternoon and floating contemplatively, all admirable and desirable activities. To continue with their competitive swimming, they needed to find a proper pool. That's when they joined the team at the YWCA in White Plains, the Middies, still in existence today.

This team was serious about competition, headed by Coach Warren Beaulieu and included two Olympians.

They swam indoors for the winter, and moved to a private club with a large outdoor facility for the summers. The Hepworth clan was again welcomed as a beneficial addition to the team. This helped Linda acclimate to her new life. The familiarity of the practices made adjustments easier and introduced her to new friends right away.

Competitive swimmers constitute a family throughout the United States. It is a stable connection understood by each member that brings a sense of understanding and camaraderie regardless of the locale. Linda believes this is true throughout the world as well, as international swimming meets bring many divergent people peaceably together for the common cause of swimming. Swimmers relate to each other, even if their love of the sport is the only common denominator.

As in Florida, each afternoon after school was spent at the pool for a two-hour practice. Fortunately Jeri was now old enough to drive everyone back and forth, taking the burden off their mother. The long, daily practices were intense because this new group was so serious. Again, most weekends were spent at meets. This meant heading to bed early on Friday night, getting up at the crack of dawn on Saturday, eating, packing and taking off to wherever the meet was held. By the time the family returned home on Saturday, and sometimes Sunday evening, they still had homework that was due Monday morning. This schedule did not leave much time for the Hepworths to get into mischief. They were just too tired.

Those early days of serious competition honed Linda for the fatigue she's feeling now. She is swimming through it, like she's always done. Keep going, she tells herself. Another lap completed, as she swims under the backstroke flags, sees the number 15, and begins her next turn. She is now three quarters of the way through.

Deep breath, stroke, stroke, somersault, push-off...

FREESTYLE *LAP SIXTEEN*

Rules are rules and the judge's decision stands.

Stroke, stroke, breathe…

Oh dear, Linda did not start that last flip turn in the right position. She was too close to the wall and her bottom got stuck out of the water. It stayed there for what seemed like seconds while she concentrated on getting her feet in the right position for a push-off. That must have looked funny if anyone was watching. She knows the importance of each flip turn, and she probably lost some time there.

She had a similar mishap on a turn at another meet. Again, flipping too close to the wall, she had to tighten into a small ball to prevent her legs from going over the edge of the pool. Everyone noticed, or so it seemed. Afterwards, Coach asked if she had scraped her nose. Now that's a tight turn! She'll wait and see what Sharlene has to say about this one, when she's finished… and no doubt there will be even more time spent on turns at her practices.

Besides anyone noticing, was there photographic

evidence? Today everybody seems to have a camera ready; she has no way of knowing if she's on film. Cameras are good to help swimmers see their strokes. Linda has been filmed at practice as well as in competitions to see her strengths as well as spot some areas that need help. For her, these films are not easy to watch. While she pictures herself doing everything exactly as Coach has told her, sometimes the reality of the film shows a different story, as above.

Recently in practice, Sharlene was helping Linda with her turns and noticed her shoulders were not level as she was coming into the wall. This particular problem could be the cause of a disqualification (DQ) in the butterfly or the breaststroke. The turns have to be made using two hands, simultaneously. If the shoulders are not level and this translates to the hands not touching on the same horizontal plane, it can appear to the judges that only one hand touched. Linda was appreciative of the observation.

She thought she was coming in straight, envisioning her turn perfectly, but in reality, she was not doing it perfectly. The judges don't care how you think you are swimming. They care about what they see, a level two-handed touch, or the swimmer is handed a piece of paper when they finish their event. That would be the dreaded yellow notice of disqualification. The judges' decisions are final.

At a recent meet, Linda spent the day near the announcer's booth. It was interesting to watch the process of running the meet, including the delivery of many dreaded yellow DQ papers. Sometimes an infraction is obvious, such as an improper one-handed touch in the breaststroke or the butterfly. Linda's witnessed that and seen the official raise his arm signifying a DQ, but mostly could only guess at what these disqualifications were for. Possibly someone did not stay on their back  during a backstroke turn, or maybe took too many strokes under water on a breaststroke start. Linda has attended a few meetings of the Rules Committee of the USMS and was fascinated by the specific details of each rule of the sport. To maintain the integrity and fairness of each race, the officials cannot afford to be lenient. The Rule Book is consulted and the rules are upheld.

When a man dove into the pool way before his race was supposed to start, it got everyone's attention. He climbed out, spoke to the starting judge and got

got back onto the block. Apparently he wasn't disqualified because they had not yet said "Take your mark." Only after that command, must the swimmer be completely stationary—no movement.

One of Linda's friends got disqualified because his arms were in motion before the starting buzzer. Technically, he had "commenced" his start too early. Her friend went on to explain that he and that particular DQ official swim in the same pool. When the two men saw each other at practice, there was a friendly mention of the DQ, but rules are rules and the decision stands.

One brand new teammate was at her first meet

and made two mistakes. Luckily for her, the judges missed them. Linda was glad. She was a novice and getting disqualified may have thwarted any pleasure and dampened her enthusiasm for swimming. Linda has seen other infractions that the officials missed. A racing breaststroker made a forbidden one-handed touch. She gasped with concern, but the turn official was watching another swimmer and did not catch it.

Disqualifications in relays happen quite a bit; the starts can be tricky. You don't want too much hesitation or loss of time between swimmers, but going off too early, making a jump start, is a lot worse than a slow time. It disqualifies the whole relay. Sometimes the swimmers don't know what happened until everything is over and they're told by the officials. But other times, the early take-off is obvious and a loud groan goes through the crowd.

There was a very public disqualification at the FINA (Fédération Internationale de Natation) World Championship Swimming meet held in Barcelona in 2008. Kevin Cordes made a jump start for his breaststroke lap of the 4x100 Medley relay. Linda learned after that incident that there is an allowance of .03 seconds on relay starts. Cordes had gone off .04 ahead, thereby disqualifying the whole relay. What a terrible let-down, and the whole world saw it!

Linda recently attended an annual meeting of the Pacific Masters, the regional group of the USMS encompassing the western states. There were elections of officers held, including one man who had been nominated to be the Chairman for the following year. He looked familiar but Linda could not place him until he spoke to the crowd. John King stated the reasons he wanted the job and then listed his qualifications. There was a murmur throughout the room when he mentioned that he was presently the DQ official at the meets, and if he had given any of the voting swimmers a yellow slip at any of the meets, please try to forget that and vote for him anyway. He won the election; apparently swimmers don't hold grudges.

Here's the wall again; deep breath, stroke, stroke, somersault, push-off...

FREESTYLE *LAP SEVENTEEN*

She reasoned that she could do
almost anything, if it's only one lap.

Stroke, stroke, breathe...

Linda's plan was to speed up at lap number 16, but she was caught off guard and became distracted by her flubbed flip turn. 100 yards to go in this race, if she wants to step up her pace, now's the time. To accomplish this, she has to really start kicking, not only keeping the beat, but kicking harder and faster. This is taking a lot of energy; her legs are complaining. Very tired, she hopes her effort will make a difference. She can't see her sister now. Looking for tangible proof that her strategy is helping, Linda will check as Jeri passes by again to see if she's gained any distance. Kick, kick, kick...

The kick that goes with the freestyle is the flutter kick. However, most fast swimmers do a few dolphin kicks coming out of each turn to keep the initial push-off momentum going. Incorporating a bit of the butterfly stroke into freestyle is intriguing to Linda. Freestyle was the first and easiest stroke that she learned to swim, and the butterfly was the last. Though especially hard to master, she loves to envision the butterfly stroke in her mind's eye. It may be the most difficult stroke to swim, but is undoubtedly the most beautiful to watch when performed correctly.

Butterfly, as a competitive stroke in swimming, was first seen in the 1956 Olympics. Prior to those Games, there were only three strokes: freestyle, backstroke and breaststroke. The underwater recovery of the breaststroke was deemed too slow and inefficient. A solution to the problem was to recover the arms simultaneously over the water, mimicking the wings of a butterfly. This method proved to be faster. When the newly choreographed "dolphin fishtail kick" was added, the modern butterfly stroke was born: hence the phrase, "breaststroke begat butterfly."

Again, kicking is the key because it takes a strong kick to power this stroke. To begin the butterfly, the swimmer's arms reach out in a Y pattern. The chest is lowered slightly, which naturally raises the butt up in the air. *Wait a minute. Someone's butt is up in the air again?* There appears to be a theme emerging. As funny as that sounds, it is the right way to maintain the pattern of butterfly. Both arms pull down simultaneously and the hips are lowered to meet them. This action pushes the torso back up, bringing the shoulders above the surface to make it easier for the forward arm swing. The fish-tail, or dolphin kick, propels the swimmer's body forward, beginning the cycle again. Getting the rhythm is the key. When Linda swims the butterfly, she can sense when she's doing it correctly, making her feel powerful. But soon she has to stop, as it is very tiring.

That's why she especially enjoys swimming the 100-yard Individual Medley (IM), which is one lap each of the four strokes. The event starts off with one lap of butterfly. Maybe the thinking behind that decision was to do the hardest stroke first and get it over with, and the dive off the blocks with the three or four kicks underwater, make it a shortened lap at that! That's the way Linda likes to swim the butterfly.

When Linda swam at the Nationals in 2009, reviving her family's famous relay, she had the added opportunity to swim some individual events. Registering for the meet meant a decision of what to swim; she considered the 100 IM. *Why not? I might as well try.* She was certain she could execute all four strokes, one lap each. At the time, she reasoned that she could do almost anything, if it's only one lap.

But when it came time to actually swim, she was so nervous about the butterfly leg of the event that she sat by herself a full hour before the race, trying to relax and think positively to ward off the anxiety. Her sister Jodie saw that her fear was almost debilitating and of-

fered to secretly step into her place, and swim the event for her. What a kind soul. However, this was Linda's feat to accomplish and hers alone.

When her heat was called up, Linda stepped up to the blocks, knees shaking. She was again comforted by the sight of her family gathered at the end of her lane to cheer her on. "Take your mark" and she dove in. Dolphin kick, kick, kick, arms out of the water, swing forward, pull down, kick, swing forward…She was doing it!

At the end of her lane, having three more laps in

the event, she unprofessionally stopped for a second to joyfully exclaim to her family. She had gotten through her feared one lap of butterfly. "Go! Go!" Her family yelled. "Keep going!" She pushed off onto her back for the backstroke leg, then a lap of breaststroke, finishing with a strong freestyle. She placed 13th in her age group, which was her best event of the day. Yeah! She still loves the 100 IM.

Linda recently watched a teammate do 100 meters of butterfly in a meet. He is an excellent swimmer and sometimes steps in as coach and took an unconventional approach. He did three strokes with his arms, dolphin kicked three times, then three strokes, then three kicks, etc. He swam the whole race like that, conserving his energy. He made certain to remain in a symmetrical position the whole way, insuring his stroke was legal. He later told Linda that even though he had done it many times, he was a bit intimidated by the race, which is why he swam it that way. Even the best swimmers have their moments of doubt.

At the 2009 Nationals, there was a noteworthy moment: a heat of young men in the 200 butterfly. One had a beautiful stroke and was fast, moving easily ahead of the other swimmers early in the race. After 6 laps, he started slowing up, showing some fatigue. He continued on, but by the last lap he was literally limping home. His arms were barely coming out of the water. Linda saw how tired he was, yet he persevered as best he could. He did get disqualified because a rule

of butterfly is that the arms must recover completely above the water, and at the end he certainly was having difficulty doing that. The other swimmers caught up with him and beat him to the finish. Oh, the disappointment.

The announcer understood, and said to the crowd, "The 200 butterfly is not an easy race. Give it up for those who tried." At one of the meetings of the Pacific Masters, someone asked the board if they would consider a special accommodation for anyone who swam the 200 butterfly. A cash award was suggested, but the idea only received a laugh and did not go to a vote. Linda is not sure that even a cash award would be enough to coax her into attempting such a swim.

For the truly brave butterfly swimmers, there's a local annual meet that ends with a very unusual event: 1650 yards of butterfly. That's 66 laps of butterfly! There is a time limit involved. The swimmers must complete the race in 45 minutes. About a dozen volunteers step up each year to test their stamina and resolve. Linda's brother Mark does the butterfly. He once told her, "If you want to earn a medal (make the top 10) in the Nationals, do the 200 butterfly. Very few people can do it." She had responded, "You're right, but I'm not one of them!"

Stop daydreaming, Linda! You're not doing the difficult butterfly. You're doing freestyle, and trying to build speed. Kick, kick, kick.

And here's the counter telling her she's finished 17 laps. She's so happy to see it each time that it's getting to be her friend. Deep breath, stroke, stroke, somersault, push-off…

FREESTYLE *LAP EIGHTEEN*

Being a lifeguard was the first job for many swimmers.

Stroke, stroke, breathe …

Linda relaxes into the rhythmic strokes again, sees her sister ahead of her, and chuckles to herself about the concept of catching up. Jeri was always ahead of Linda, a year older, the outgoing one, popular in high school, while Linda was more introspective and quiet. Jeri got the summer jobs first, and then Linda stepped into the position the next summer. Linda used to boast about the fact that she never applied for a job, she just took Jeri's hand-me-downs, making life easier for her.

The first summer job was as a lifeguard at their swim club, Rocky Ledge Swimming Association. Jeri was the oldest of the five siblings, and so was offered the head lifeguard position. This made sense, since the whole family had been spending every summer day for the past three years at this pool. They started each weekday morning with a 2-hour competitive team practice, then stayed the rest of the day at the pool relaxing, casually swimming, playing cards with her

Middie teammates and reading during the hot, muggy summer afternoons. This was the same team that swam together indoors during the winter at the YWCA.

The Rocky Ledge Swim Club featured a competition pool and deep diving well. Diving boards had not been outlawed yet, and there were three of them, starting at one meter high. The top tier was three meters high that Olympic divers use today. During those summers spent at the pool, only the brave ones jumped, or dove, off the three-meter board. Linda could count on one hand the times she ventured off the top, usually on a dare, after much urging from her teammates. Three meters is a long way down with the possibility of a painful landing if she wasn't completely streamlined in entry, not to mention the embarrassment of diving poorly in front of her friends.

The team became a large family unit since they spent so much time with each other, and the Hepworths were a big part of it all. Spending the day at the pool became a way of life. The family practically kept the snack bar financially afloat by themselves. Their mother always packed a healthy lunch for them, sandwiches, apples, carrots and celery, but the allure of French fries, ice cream sandwiches and Nutty Buddy ice cream cones that were for sale, was too strong to resist.

Often on the drive home in the early evening hours, Linda saw folks out walking, fully dressed in the sweltering heat. She thought she was so lucky to be able to have spent the day wearing only a bathing suit and being able to jump in the water to cool off whenever she felt like it. Many of her high school friends got summer jobs in grocery stores or offices where they had to have a professional wardrobe. When Jeri and Linda were hired as lifeguards, they spent the whole day outside, dressed in their favorite attire: bathing suits.

Being a lifeguard was the first job for many swimmers. The Red Cross organization trained them in life saving techniques and water safety. The fact that they were already spending time at the pool each day made it a natural progression. Linda worked as a lifeguard at Rocky Ledge the next summer, following her sister's footsteps with their brother Mark taking up the role when his time came. The younger sisters each stepped up in turn.

The summer after high school, she took another position previously held by her sister, as a lifeguard at a local hotel. Laws require a lifeguard to be on premises, even though the pool was small and usually sparsely used. The manager told Linda more than once that he was not happy with the fact that he was paying her to "sit there all day." What

the manager did not take onto account was the fact that Linda only sat a bit of the day. She was responsible for the upkeep of the pool: keeping it free of debris, backwashing the filters and setting the PH levels correctly. As with any other job, there was always plenty to do, sweeping, keeping the place tidy and inviting to the hotel guests. Responsible Linda went about her duties and tried to dismiss the negative feedback from her manager. After all, it was only a temporary job; she looked forward to starting college in the fall.

That temporary summer position turned out to be a turning point for Linda, one she will never forget, especially the July 4th weekend. Contrary to the notion that she just sat around, her job as lifeguard that day was anything but uneventful. The hotel was full of vacationing families, young children dangerously running with wet bare feet, ignoring the NO RUNNING signs painted all around the pool. Women in their flowered bathing caps were wading in the shallow end. There was a lot of commotion and activity. Many non-swimmers were at the pool for the first and probably only time all summer. Linda had to rescue two hotel guests from the water that day.

The first was a small child who panicked when he found himself in deep water. Linda used a long handled hook to reach out to the boy. He had been scared but changed his demeanor right away as he happily got pulled back to the shallow end. For him, it was a Disneyland ride getting pulled along and he wanted to do it again. Linda had to tell him that it was for emergency purposes only, and not for play.

The second rescue, although successful, was not so happy. A woman was wading in the shallow end with her young son on her shoulders. The child was splashing water, kicking and having fun as his mother slowly made her way into the middle of the pool. Linda saw that she was heading toward much deeper water, nearing the downward slope and her feet were starting to slide. She seemed to be having trouble getting her footing; her mouth was very close to going under water. From Linda the Lifeguard's point of view, things were turning dangerous. The long hook would not suffice here. Because of the commotion caused by her playful son, the woman would not be able to reach out and grab it.

Lifeguard techniques explain that during a rescue, it is imperative for the lifeguard to stay at a safe distance from a drowning person. An immediate response is to grab onto anything, even someone who is trying to save them, resulting in the original victim taking the lifeguard down with them. In this instance, Linda got into the deep end, sculled herself forward and used her feet to gently push the woman back into the shallow water. It was a bit surprising that the woman did not thank her, or even seem to acknowledge the trouble in which she had been, or that she had literally been saved! At the time Linda justified the woman's silence; maybe she was just embarrassed. She went home that evening proud of her quick thinking in the situation, using a clever and inventive technique. No one had drowned on her watch.

Therefore, she was quite surprised when she arrived at work the next day and was called into the manager's office for a scolding. The woman had complained that she had been manhandled. The manager knew only the story told by his hotel guest. Linda tried to explain, but he was more concerned with the guest's point of view.

After that day, Linda started having nightmares of drowning victims. In the dreams, she could see people struggling in the water, but her arms seemed stuck somehow and she could not reach out to help. These nightmares were very real, and she worried about the huge responsibility being a lifeguard put on her young shoulders: someone's life. That was the last lifeguard job that Linda held. She decided to pursue a safer career; she's a waitress now and serves dinner. The worst thing that can happen, if she does not do her job correctly, is someone misses a meal. However, during her long career as a restaurant server, she prevented a woman from getting burned when her hair got too close to a candle flame, immediately catching fire, and she has successfully used the Heimlich Maneuver twice. Linda figures that she cannot escape her destiny as she navigates her way through this life.

Another lap accomplished! Deep breath, stroke, stroke, somersault, push-off...

FREESTYLE *LAP NINETEEN*

Now is the time to take any reserved energy and build to a sprint.

Stroke, stroke, breathe…

Linda hears a loud bell ringing especially for her, signifying that she has only 2 more laps to swim. Besides the counters at the far end of the pool lowering their plastic numbers for the swimmers to see, the timing officials also count the laps and ring the bell for each swimmer for the last 50 yards. It is a welcome sound. She has completed 18 of the 20 laps.

Now is the time to take any reserved energy and build to a sprint, as best she can. She can barely see her sister now. Jeri is well ahead of her. Linda's only thoughts are about kicking hard, pulling as much water back with each stroke and moving ahead as fast as she can. *Boy, this is hard*. She's really tired and having difficulty keeping up her speed. She has to tell herself that this is not the time to slow down. She remembers the mantra: *picture yourself swimming this race effortlessly and with perfect technique,* and recites it a few times to distract her mind from the fatigue. She chuckles a bit at the idea that she is swimming perfectly, and it certainly is not effortless, but there's nothing wrong with setting high goals. Even if she does not exactly live up to them, setting achievement goals is the first step to actually accomplishing the dream. Successfully envisioning an event is half the battle.

A swimmer's joke: The coach is telling the team to envision and a smart ass yells out that he can only envision the cheeseburger he's going to be enjoying after he's done with practice.

The mind is very powerful; the envisioning can go both ways. Negative thoughts and doubts can also affect the outcome. Linda recalled a relatively bad day at a meet. She says relatively, because any day at a swimming meet is already a step ahead. But that particular day, Linda was not swimming her fastest times, wasn't placing very well, and felt more and more defeated as the day progressed. Seeing this, Coach used supportive comments to help shrug off the defeatist thinking: "Go to your happy place." "Don't let it bother you, there will be other events." She told Linda, "Don't take the competitions so seriously; they should be fun and enjoyable." This is often easier said than done, excellent advice if one takes it.

As a side note, the best part of that negative day turned out to be the ribbons. She did not earn any coveted blues for 1st place, no 2nd place red ones. At the end of the meet, Linda had a fistful of rainbow colored ribbons: cheery yellows for her 4th place finishes,

deep greens for 5th and a bold orange handed out for 7th place. Linda remarked that the beauty of the colorful assortment made her feel better.

The power of mind over body made itself known at another meet as well. She had taken time off and had not been to many practices leading up to this particular day. She told Coach that she was just going to take it easy. She knew she could swim the events, so she was going to do her best. Linda surprised everyone, including herself, by swimming her fastest times in almost every race, because she was calm and not stressed. Unknowingly, she had called upon the power of the relaxed, yet focused mind. She had swum with a positive mental attitude.

Before she began this 500, she was watching the heat before her. In particular Linda was watching the woman in Lane 1, the lane she's in now. At first, she just saw someone swimming along and coming towards the end of the long race going a bit slower than the others which boosted Linda's confidence. *It's not that important how fast I swim. The fact that I'm giving it an honest effort is what really matters...and that lady's lucky, she's almost done!* Just then the announcer called out, "Give it up for Maurine Kornfeld , 92 years young in Lane 1, just finishing 20 laps of the pool. The crowd erupted into applause. When she made her final touch, she beamed with pride and waved to the crowd in acknowledgement. In 2018, Maurine was inducted into the International Masters Swimming Hall of Fame. Accepting her award, she entertained the audience, "If you can't out-swim them, out-live them." *Words of wisdom — if Maurine can do it, so can I.*

Linda feels grateful that US Masters Swimming provides these professional platforms. She has learned so much about life, about the benefits of hard work and discipline, about trials and triumphs, all from the rituals of practice, teamwork and competitions. The sport has also introduced her to some wonderful people.

Rowdy Gaines won the freestyle in the 1984 Olympics, is still breaking his own records and Linda had the opportunity to watch him race a 50-yard freestyle. The buzzer sounded and ten strong, fast men dove into the pool. There was a sound that could only be described as thunderous: water splashing, feet kicking, arms swinging, all over in under 20 seconds. It was hard to discern the order of finish amongst all the splash and excitement, but the electronics proved that Rowdy had indeed touched first, keeping his winning streak alive. Linda was astounded. She swims that event in 32 seconds. To watch these men complete two lengths so fast was just unbelievable. These are amazing, inspiring people. And she's right there with them.

Swim Linda, swim as fast as you can. The plastic counter has no number 19 on it, only a large red square, signifying the last turn. *It's time to take it home.* She gulps in a deep breath and flips over. *Push off strongly!*

FREESTYLE *LAP TWENTY*

*The black line has been with her the whole race, and
now she's following it towards home.*

Stroke, stroke, breathe…

She's breathing every stroke, kicking as hard
as she can, calling on all her reserved energy. Gone
are the leisurely reflections; no more daydreaming,
no more looking around: just one more lap: stroke,
breathe, stroke, gulping as much air as possible. All
Coach's words come tumbling through her brain: keep
your head low in the water, stretch your arms long,
pull down directly; kick strongly. She's spending so
much time trying to maintain these concepts that this
lap seems to go faster than the rest. The black line has
been with her the whole race, and now she's following it towards home. She likens herself to the horse
that seems sluggish on the way out of the barn but
has surprising strength and stamina on the way back.
Soon, she sees the flags nearing, and then she's under
them. *Don't breathe after the flags,* Linda remembers, so
she puts her head down, kicks with all she's got, sees
the "T" bar coming closer…

She stretches out her right arm, extending her shoulder as far as she can and makes a decisive final touch at the wall. She raises her head and immediately takes a big gulp of air. Her chest is pounding. She did it, 20 laps!

<hr/>

Her face breaks into a wide smile. She can't help it, and she can't hide it. She's smiling as hard as she can, trying to catch her breath. As a habit, she glances up at the scoreboard. There is a time recorded, but it does not really register. All she knows is that she's done. She's accomplished what she set out to do. Jeri is grinning too, having finished a few seconds before and already has her goggles and swim cap off.

This is the best part of any swimming event—when it's over, even though that doesn't seem like a good thing to say. It sounds as if she doesn't like competing, but it's not like that. It's just that once it's over, all the anxiety is gone. She feels tired for sure, but the sense of complete satisfaction and pride sweep away the fatigue. All the swimmers feel it and give each other knowing smiles. Linda looks at her sister, leans over to her in the next lane and they hug, feeling the hard plastic lane line between them. Linda has to wait a few minutes to make sure everyone in her heat has finished before she can move out of her lane, find the ladder and climb out of the pool. This gives her a chance to try and slow her breathing. The swimmers all wait for the whistle, giving the signal to exit the pool.

Still breathing hard, she follows Jeri towards the ladder at the edge of the pool, taking off her goggles and her cap. She ducks underwater to cool her face. All the hard exercise has heated her up, but she didn't feel it until she stopped swimming. Another dip to smooth her hair but she does so quickly, breathing too hard to be under the water for very long. Some of the swimmers get out of the pool by hoisting themselves at the end of the lanes. Linda isn't going to attempt that. She's exhausted, and even with the help of the ladder, finds it an effort to pull herself up and out. The whistle blows again as the next group of women step up on the blocks behind her and Linda hears, "Take your mark." The meet is moving right along, as the buzzer sends the next group into the pool with the familiar splash of entry.

On the pool deck, Linda stands dripping wet next to her sister as they both catch their breath and watch the next heat of swimmers. She has the urge to stop everyone passing by and excitedly tell them that she has just swum the 500-yard freestyle, in the Nationals! Almost involuntarily, she blurts out, "I just finished the 500!" Those who heard her responded with understanding nods. The whole family had come down on the pool deck to cheer and congratulate them both. Almost in another world, still dreamy and moving on auto-pilot, Linda acknowledges them and continues to follow Jeri to the other pool to do their warm-down laps. She jumps in and swims a few wonderful, leisurely laps in the warm-down pool. *Oh, that feels good.* Her body and spirit are buoyed by the water calmly surrounding her, caressing and comforting her. The previous nervousness and anxiety have transferred into a feeling of complete exhilaration. *This is why I swim.*

According to Sharlene, these laps in the warm-down pool are necessary after any race. The slow exercise helps muscles exhaust any lactic acid that's built up from the strenuous activity. But to Linda, it's just another moment in time, when the water is calling to her for relaxation. *Don't get too comfortable.* Her mind quickly reminds her that she is at a National swimming meet and the day has just begun and she should be using this time to prepare for her next event, the 200 backstroke. With that thought, she flips onto her back and does a few laps of backstroke. Her arms feel good and strong as she pulls down, using different muscles than in the freestyle. After practicing two backstroke flip turns, she climbs out of the pool. She figures she has about an hour to rest, so she finds her way to the team tent.

FOUR

~~~~~~~~~~~~~~~~~~~~~~~~~~~~~~~~~~~~~~~

Will she swim another 500? She's too fatigued
to think about that right now

While she was doing all that daydreaming, Linda
swam a consistent 45 seconds for each 50 yards. Her
last 50 with the extra kicking, was 42 seconds, bringing her time to 7 minutes and 24 seconds. It was a
good swim, said Sharlene, and it was fast enough to
earn her 11th place. Her sister Jeri had been faster
and won another well-deserved medal with 8th place.

Surprisingly, Linda was not upset about just missing a medal. She had never swum the event before
and did not know how she would fare. There is no
place for bad sportsmanship or any negative feelings
in Masters swimming. The idea is to set a goal and
achieve it, and Linda had done just that. She felt very
accomplished, and there certainly is no shame in 11th
place in the Nationals. She was elated for herself and
very happy for her sister. She is not unfamiliar with
the infamous 11th place finish. At a recent meet Linda
swam 50 meters freestyle, with her best personal time
of 35.78, placing 11th. Tenth place, for the medal, was

35.70. Eight hundredths of a second difference! She mentioned afterwards that she could have done better, if she just didn't breathe during the race!

All her teammates and coach congratulate her and give her some pointers for the next time. There will be a next time? Will she do that again, swim another 500? She's too fatigued to think about that right now. There are questions about her time and if she had any mishaps to report. The small issue with her cap almost coming off was too uninteresting to mention, but Linda proudly told her teammates about getting her butt stuck in the air on turn 16. And she repeatedly mentioned to anyone who would listen how good it feels after the event.

Linda is tired and wants to rest before her next race. She lays out on one of the sleeping bags and closes her eyes. Linda will spend time with her family later. They understand that she needs this down time between events. Her family is still in the grandstands watching the meet. Her mother in particular, seems very 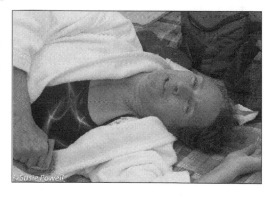 interested in the proceedings. Having spent so much time watching her children compete, she is familiar with all the events and what's going on. Rather than sit comfortably in the shade with Linda's sisters, their mom is standing in the hot sun, leaning against a railing, very close to the pool. It soon became clear why she was so fascinated when she turned her head and mentioned that the older men who swim don't seem to have paunches...

While she's resting after her long race, Linda thinks about the old family days. It was their mother who took the kids on the daily runs to practice. She was a teacher with a full time job, but was able to attend all the practices and the meets on weekends. She spent so many hours at the pool that she took up knitting to help pass the time. Ultimately she became an official. That meant helping with the paperwork, the recordkeeping and the timing of the events. Just like today, Linda's mom had always been there. Over the years, she's witnessed all the thrills of victory as well as the agonies of defeat.

Their dad wasn't as involved when it came to the family sport. He heard about all the excitement after the fact, over the dinner table. He was busy working and being responsible for all the opportunities the family had growing up. As a young family man, he was a hard worker on the Hepworth Apple Farm with his father and brother; hence the close living arrangements of the extended family, which Linda considered a blessing. She looks back on those family times with particular fondness.

When he wasn't working, Linda's dad liked to have fun, joining the family in the pool whenever he had a chance. Linda's mother recently reminded her of a particular scary water incident when Dad was teaching the young children how to swim. He was holding Jeri above the water trying to give her some confidence. He was dipping her in and out, reassuring her, teaching her how to float. He then looked down and saw that Linda was submerged. He dropped Jeri into the water, to quickly grab Linda and bring her safely to the surface. That really scared Jeri. Consoling apologetic words from Dad calmed everyone down. Today you'd never know that these siblings went through some trials of their own, and could have easily grown up wary of the water.

Now that Linda has finished the 500, most of her anxiety has dispersed through exertion. She can relax a bit, so she takes a few deep breaths and looks around her. She is lying comfortably on a sleeping bag under a canopy amidst a sea of canopies. Hundreds of people are doing the same. They're resting, preparing themselves for their upcoming races. Coaches are giving instructions and keeping an eye on the progression of events. Sharlene always lets the team know when a fellow Mud Shark is in the water, "Greg's doing breaststroke now," or "Don's up, doing his 200 IM. Let's go watch and cheer him on!" Linda takes in the whole atmosphere of this meet. She can't believe she's here again, immersed in the world of competitive swimming. It's like bringing her youth back, if she doesn't look too closely in the mirror...

FIVE

Reviving the famous Hepworth relay...

Linda can thank Jeri for reintroducing her to competitive swimming as an adult. It was 2008, when she phoned with the invitation to join the family of Masters Swimmers. When the call came through, there was something positive, even cheerful, in the sound of the ring tone.

It was certainly surprising to hear from her sister at that time of day, early afternoon in the middle of the week. Normally Linda would be at work, but the restaurant where she had worked for 18 years suddenly shut down. She lost her lunchtime job. Letting the news sink in personally was harder than she'd anticipated, talking about it was not easy. She had no answer for the inevitable questions, "What will you do now? What are your plans?" Perhaps Linda was just hoping for some sorely needed good news.

She knew that she had been working too much, not allowing time for life affirming, recreational activities. She still had her evening job, so financial issues were not a concern. This unexpected emptiness in her schedule was taking some time to get used to. She'd planned to take a few weeks and consider her options. But right now, the phone was ringing.

"I'm so glad you're home! I have great news. Do you remember that I told you I'd been swimming extra hard at my practices? Well, I've qualified for the Nationals, and the rules say that if one person qualifies, they can build a relay.

"Linda, I want to get our family swimming together again and revive our famous Hepworth relay at the Nationals! I've been talking to Tracy and Jodie, and they are on board with the idea. The meet will be held in Fresno, California, close to where you live. It will be great! It's going to be on Mother's Day weekend, too. Let's make it a surprise for Mom! What do you think?" When she heard those words, "the famous Hepworth relay," Linda knew just what her sister was referring to, the exciting summer of 1968.

A few months before that phone call, Jeri had helped their mother move to a new home, and in the

process of packing up, came across the old plaque commemorating the winning relay. She told Linda that she had plans to take the plaque to an engraver to have the new date of 2009 inscribed if the idea panned out.

That call was the pivotal event that brought Linda back into competitive swimming after a 40-year hiatus. She took it as an omen. Perhaps this was why her time had been freed up. She marveled at the idea that all things happen for a reason. There was no hesitation. Just like their relay event in 1968, Linda considered this new endeavor something she could not miss. Her excitement grew as she considered the prospect of swimming competitively again and sharing this experience with her family.

Linda thought back to all those years when she wasn't swimming regularly. Her life schedule did not allow for much aquatic activity. She always owned a bathing suit as a natural part of her wardrobe, and swam on occasion for fun. But a leisurely dip in a friend's pool is certainly not the same as regular practices and competitions. What her sister had just suggested required some serious effort: find somewhere to practice, get in shape. What an amazing idea! Something she had not thought about for so many years, competitive swimming, now front and center of her world.

Their brother Mark had been involved with Masters Swimming for a few years, qualified and was going to be swimming in the meet. Over the years, he had repeatedly invited his sisters to join. He was sure they would enjoy the competitions. Jeri had joined him and was obviously doing well: she had qualified for the Nationals. At that time, the interest was just not there for Linda, Tracy or Jodie, but Jeri's suggestion changed everything and brought everybody back into the fold.

As soon as she got off the phone, Linda started a search and made a few phone calls. This was October, and the meet was in May. She had six months to get ready; plenty of time, she thought. There was a lovely tennis club in town with a small pool, only 20 yards in length, but it would do. She joined the club and started swimming three to four times a week. The length of the pool was a concern, because regulation meets are held in 25-yard pools. Practicing in a smaller pool is a slight disadvantage, as the body becomes accustomed to the distance. So Linda kept that in mind and swam extra laps to compensate for the shorter yardage. She wanted to perform well.

At first, as expected, she had trouble swimming one lap, becoming easily out of breath. But soon the muscle memories of her younger days came right back, and she was doing 100 laps, and more. She stayed in close contact with Tracy and Jodie who lived nearby, and they catalogued each other's progress. They studied new techniques illustrated on the internet and shared the information. For example, there was a new backstroke turn and a different way to swim breaststroke, allowing for the head to completely submerge. That used to be illegal. Things had certainly changed in 40 years.

Linda, Tracy and Jodie had each gotten off to a

good start with their training. So when they met for practice sessions at each others' pools, rather than do a hard workout, they spent time taking pictures and chatting. There was some serious swimming, but mostly the sisters did a lot of treading water and dog paddle, so any conversation wasn't interrupted. Despite this, each sister knew this preparation time was important; they needed to swim, and swim regularly. Ultimately they got down to the business at hand. Linda felt certain they would be ready.

Besides practicing in the pool the sisters used this extra special time together to research some local restaurants, trying the many varieties of wine that Northern California has to offer. Having a couple of glasses of chardonnay after swimming is a sure way to relax. The wine was only part of it as the extra calories expended in the water gave them a terrific appetite. It was wintertime and their pools were outdoors. The water was nicely heated, but those steps out to the pool and back to the locker room were chilly, making the after-practice hot meals taste extra delicious.

When Christmas came around that year, all the family was abuzz about the big surprise for Mom. The family wanted the holiday to be special and decided to tell their mother about the upcoming joint venture. They thought that the anticipation of such a gathering would be good for her, something to look forward to, not to mention giving her bragging rights to all her friends. It was a happy Christmas with everyone appreciative of their many blessings: first, that the five siblings were all still alive, and secondly that they were all healthy enough for this endeavor. Linda sometimes thinks that her family's good health can be attributed to all those apples and oranges they ate growing up. Dad had passed away some years before, so the third blessing was that their Mother was still around to see the magic happen again.

The months passed quickly. May was approaching. Soon would come the time of reckoning. The family planned to make a full weekend of it. The meet was going to be held at a state-of-the-art aquatic facility in Clovis, a suburb of Fresno, California. The Hepworths reserved three rooms at a hotel close to the competition, chosen mostly because the brochure mentioned the presence of a pool. It's amusing to note that when the family went to these meets, spending the whole day at a pool, it was still important to them to have yet another pool available to them in the evenings for a leisurely dip after the intense competitions.

⚬⚬⚬

After so many months of anticipation and preparation, May 7th finally arrived. The first leg of Linda's journey was to travel south, pick up her two sisters, and continue on to their hotel, the pool and their destiny. The three-hour drive went by quickly with the sisters chatting, encouraging each other and agreeing how lucky they were to be in this event together. Their excitement mixed with trepidation, they wondered aloud how they would fare against the best in the nation. Linda's stomach was in turmoil with nervousness, and she assumed her sisters felt the same way. Mark told them that anxiety was part of the whole competition. Everybody feels it, to one degree or another. The trick is to channel that energy into speed.

When they arrived at the hotel, Mom, their brother Mark, and Jeri, who had organized the whole affair, were on hand to greet them. Jeri's husband Robert was there too, as he never missed any of his wife's competitions. They all had a leisurely dinner out by the pool, of course. The conversation was quiet, anticipating the upcoming events, and everyone retired early to get a good night's sleep.

SIX

~~~~~~

Linda and her family made a big splash at the meet.

"Good morning." Linda heard her mother's voice, waking her gently as she used to do before the swimming meets of her youth. "It's time to swim." Breakfast was hearty, with yogurt, bananas, eggs, bacon and potatoes. Although very nervous, Linda knew she had to eat and eat well to give her body the fuel it needed to perform. Protein snacks and fruit were all right during the meet, but she needed full sustenance to start the day off right. She'd had a constant feeling of anxiety since she started this journey, but that day the nervous twinges were exponentially higher. It was her first meet in years. It was important to swim her best because her family was counting on her. The drive from the hotel to the venue gave Linda time to try to calm down, repeating the mantra: *I can do this. I'm a swimmer.*

The 2009 USMS Short Course Summer Nationals competition was in full swing when they arrived. These championships start very early in the morning to accommodate the longer swims and the many participants. The sound of whistles and electronic starting buzzers could be heard from the parking lot. As the family entered, they saw that corporate vendors were set up all around the pools selling T-shirts, bathing suits, goggles and sport drinks. Numerous tents housed all the teams from around the United States. The bleachers were decorated with team banners and advertising posters. Linda passed right by the Mud Sharks with their toothy shark banner, not realizing they would later be a big part of her life. Six months before this, Mark's coach had kindly allowed the sisters to sign up with his team, so Linda and her family were affiliated with Team Ridglea, based in Texas.

Two adjoining pools were in use for the competition, each 25 yards long; the set-up was very easy to navigate. The odd numbered events, Event 1, 3, 5 etc. were swum in one pool, and the even numbered events, 2, 4, etc. were in the other. This is an efficient way to run a large meet, as it prevents a hold up due to one swimmer being a bit more leisurely than the others. Everybody gets to swim at their own pace and finish without the anxious feeling that the whole meet is being held up just for them. However, this is the Nationals. There are minimum times required to qualify, so if there are any hold-ups, it is usually because of electronic equipment or clerical problems, not due to any slow swimmers. Similar to most meets, there was a third pool for warming up before a swim, and warming down. That pool stayed busy with swimmers all day long.

Linda and her family made a big splash at the meet. Everyone within earshot heard of their family's trek to get there, involving all five siblings swimming together for the first time in 41 years. It was Mother's Day weekend, close to their mother's birthday. There was a lot to celebrate.

Jodie's husband Bruce had T-shirts printed up with a fictitious family code of arms and the words Hepworth Swimming emblazoned in red. A few swimmers asked where Hepworth was. Linda pointed out her brother's whereabouts, getting quizzical responses before she realized the swimmers were mistaking their family name with a locale or a swim club. For good luck, she still brings that T-shirt to competitions, as well as all the family reunions and gatherings. It is getting a bit threadbare, but the sentiments are still strong.

Besides repeatedly telling their story, the Hepworths stood out with theatrics. Tracy is a dancer, involved in many dramatic productions. She had recently performed in a Tina Turner

Review and thought it a brilliant idea to bring along the sequined mini dresses she'd worn. Four dresses, all different colors, were reminiscent of shiny mermaid skin. Mark used a glittery sash as a headband; he didn't want to be left out of the fun.

Other teams near them appreciated all the commotion coming from the Hepworths. When the mini dresses appeared, one team called the sisters over and handed them four, old-fashioned bathing caps topped with colorful rubber flowers not seen since the fifties. They were a perfect accessory to the Tina Turner dresses. The caps came from the Flower Power Team of Santa Rosa, California, just north of Linda's home. They had previously used them to make their own splash at the meets.

Linda knew a few of the swimmers on the team, including her friend Cassandra, a very fast swimmer. She's in a younger age group, so the two friends are not in direct competition. By coincidence, Linda and

Cassandra were wearing the exact same bathing suit. With all the designs and color variants the different companies come up with every year, this was something. *Great minds think alike*, thought Linda.

Linda and her siblings were having a blast. Their mom told them to be careful, lest they seem a bit disrespectful of the solemnity of the competition. But nobody seemed to mind the frivolity.

When their event number was called, the four Hepworth sisters wore the colorful dresses over to the blocks to swim their relay. They quickly disrobed, to get ready and not delay the meet in any way. The flowered caps were exchanged for regular competition bathing caps. The plastic blooms were deemed not streamlined enough to risk swimming with them. Since they hadn't done this in a very long time, they wanted every advantage. Now they were ready to swim their 200-yard medley relay.

The long whistle blew and Tracy jumped in the water to lead off with the backstroke. Relays start with the backstroke since that stroke starts from the water. "Take your mark." Tracy used the handles on the starting block to pull her torso up out of the water and planted her feet on the wall. She gave her sisters a nod which said, "It's now or never…" With the sound of the electronic buzzer, she propelled her arched body backwards into the water.

Tracy swam her heart out, one lap up and one back. She swam quite quickly too, or so it seemed to Linda who was already up on the starting blocks, her knees shaking. She was to swim next and do the breaststroke. Linda had to make sure that Tracy touched the wall before she dove in. A common error in relays is when one swimmer dives from the blocks too early, which causes a disqualification. There it is — the touch. And Linda is off.

Good dive, good start, as she reminds herself to swim two laps of breaststroke. Sometimes in the excitement of competition, a swimmer forgets which stroke they're supposed to be doing. Linda pulls down with both arms. She uses a strong whip kick to bring herself to the surface and takes her first stroke. *Duck your head*, she tells herself like she saw on the instructional videos on the internet. *Pull down. Oh my! I'm swimming in a meet! Oh joy!* She gets to the far end, hears her family's cries of encouragement, makes a legal two-hand touch, turns around, and pushes off for her second and last lap of this event.

The breaststroke feels slow. Linda wants to swim fast, but that's not the nature of the breaststroke. She has to maintain her pattern of stroke, kick, and breathe. Her breathing is hard and regular, getting some water in her mouth. Soon she's swimming beneath the backstroke flags and the wall is approaching. She makes a two-handed touch of course, as she sees Jeri's shadow fly off the blocks above her for two laps of butterfly. Linda did not see much of Jeri's leg of the relay because she was so out of breath, concentrating only on staying out of the way. She and Tracy were "hanging out" in the lane, breathing hard and grinning from ear to ear.

Jodie was on the blocks. She waited until Jeri touched the wall, and made a beautiful dive over Linda's head. Arms racing, using a familiar freestyle stroke, soon Jodie had flipped and was heading back. She touched with a solid finish, and it was all over in a little over 2 minutes. Just like that, all done! The sisters had successfully recreated their relay, 40 years after they first emerged onto the scene of competitive swimming, and the exhilaration was overwhelming. They had been preparing for months, spent countless hours and had put so much effort into this, all for a 2 minute event. It almost defies explanation, this love of swimming.

They swam the relay in a very respectable time, but it wasn't the time that concerned any of them. Frankly, Linda cannot recall the time they swam. The only important issue was that the sisters had done it, had come back to a place from where they had started.

All those swim practices and meets, all the years led up to this moment. The feelings: happiness, relief, satisfaction rolled up together, probably never to be duplicated. The wide smiles on their happy faces said it all.

Their relay placed 12th but ended up being disqualified due to a registration mishap. They had made a mistake in the signing up process, a novice's error. The disqualification was a bit disappointing, but Linda and her sisters knew that it was not due to any lack of swimming know-how on their part. They shrugged it off, realizing that it didn't really matter. They all knew they had accomplished their goal, swimming their relay in a big competition just like they had so many years ago. God had seen it, US Masters Swimming had seen it, and their mother and their families had seen it. They still had it in them. Woo hoo! What a day!

Not only did the meet officials not mind the frivolity, the Hepworth family was selected out of more than 1000 swimmers to be interviewed for USMS *Swimmer* magazine, in the issue of July/August, 2009. It was a very complimentary article starting with the fact that brother Mark was the one who got all the sisters into the act, so to speak. They were forever immortalized.

***

While Linda has been resting and reminiscing about that wonderful day, the commotion around her has been steady. She hears Sharlene calling for all Mud Sharks to go to the pool's edge to encourage their teammates. Feeling rested enough, she stands at the pool edge with her coach and watches as Sarah swims the 100 butterfly. Linda follows each arm swing sympathetically. Sarah makes it look effortless, but when she finishes she looks up and whispers, "That was hard." Linda understood. Each event, whether it's a short or long one, takes an amazing amount of strength and stamina.

Then teammate Doug swam the 100-yard breast-stroke. A strong swimmer, he gets it done without much fanfare. Linda wonders about his easy going at-titude, not outwardly bothered by the stress of compe-tition. Could it be just a ploy to relax and swim well? Anyway, whatever method he uses, he registered an astoundingly fast time. Worth mentioning about these two swims are the equivalent times they recorded. When registering for the meet, both Sarah and Doug expected to do 1:09 for their respective events. That was their seed time, used by the officials to lay out the heats, in order of slowest to fastest. Sarah swam her 100 butterfly in 1:04, and Doug swam his 100 breast in 1:04. Each swam 5 seconds faster than their previous best times, and if swum side by side, would have tied! Those were two wonderful races for Linda to watch, noting that the last time she swam the 100-yard free, she clocked a time of 1:14. Both Sarah's butterfly and Doug's breaststroke are a lot faster than Linda's free-style. Just saying…

SEVEN

200-YARD BACKSTROKE

The terms backwards, blindly and belly up sound like someone is in distress. But all three perfectly describe swimming the backstroke.

Now it's time for Linda's second event, the 200 backstroke. She starts to get ready, physically and emotionally, to swim eight lengths of the pool. After completing 20 laps of freestyle, an event of only 8 laps is somewhat of a relief, and she's looking forward to what has recently become her favorite event. She once told herself in the middle of a 200 backstroke that she could continue on like this forever.

Linda puts on her cap, dons her dark goggles and makes her way to the appropriate pool and her designated lane. There she waits for her heat number to be called. She's watching all the other competitors as she breathes deeply, preparing her body for the upcoming exertion. When it's time, she steps up to the edge of the pool. She listens for the long whistle, the signal for the swimmers to jump into the water to start their race. The water feels cool as she leaps in, turns around and grabs the hand-holds on the starting blocks. She takes up her position: planting her feet on the wall, tilting her head back. Soon she hears the familiar words: "Take your mark." She pulls her body up, ready for the push-off. The electronic buzzer sound that has been so constant throughout the day, once again sends Linda and nine other swimmers splashing backwards into the water. With her arms up and held tightly against her head, she's trying to be an arrow moving sleekly through the water. Her event of 200-yard backstroke has begun.

BACKSTROKE *LAP ONE*

This race is eight laps and cannot be swum in a sprint.

While still underwater, she immediately starts kicking. Her right arm moves first, pulling downward to bring her body to the surface. She takes in a big gulp of air and lifts her right shoulder out of the water making it easier for her right arm to swing back up , as her left arm pulls down. Pinky first, her hand enters the water shaped like a cup so that she can catch and push as much water as possible. As her right arm pulls down, her left shoulder rises allowing her left arm to lift easily through the air to begin her next stroke. Her arms pull strongly through the water and Linda watches as they swing past her viewpoint, one at a time.

A familiar rush of adrenalin is surging through her body, compelling her to start out swimming hard and fast. She has to remind herself that this event is eight laps, a middle distance race, and cannot be swum in a sprint. *Calm down, Linda. Start out slowly.* She exhales deeply and starts to breathe regularly. Kicking is still important here, and she begins to count her kicks: 1-2-

3, 1-2-3. The pattern of her backstroke emerges.

Competing in backstroke is relatively new to Linda. She had always been the breaststroker in the family and thought that was her niche. She swam the breaststroke lap in the famous Hepworth relay, and entered breaststroke events when she returned to swimming. Breaststroke was familiar to her.

But then her brother Mark gave her the idea to try competing in the backstroke, convincing her that she would do well in it. She took his advice initially because she thought it would be easier. She could readily list the benefits: The biggest attraction to the stroke was the start; no forward dive, therefore no worry  about losing her goggles. Backstroke events start from the water, as Linda just did for this race. Another bonus, she felt more comfortable having her face out of the water, allowing for easier breathing during her race. In freestyle her head is held underwater with the long black line on the bottom of the pool her main view. She catches an occasional glimpse of the other swimmers only when she turns her head to breathe.

Linda used to think that swimming face up meant she could casually look around, scanning the sky for birds or cloud formations. But she quickly discovered that's only during recreational swimming. In competition, once the race starts, there's no time for casual looking around. Total concentration is on her race and swimming as fast as she can.

The terms backwards, blindly and belly up are usually applied when someone is in distress, but they perfectly describe swimming the backstroke. Linda swims forward, viewing only what's behind her. Even though she does not look where she's going, she's confident in her journey. Hours in her new team's regulation 25-yard pool where she now practices with the Mud Sharks, have conditioned Linda to the distance. On occasion she swims for fun at her old Tennis Club- a lap in that 20-yard pool now seems very short. She knows where she is in her lane today. She can thank the regulations of US Masters Swimming for requiring these racing courses to be uniform.

The regulations also dictate the proper, or legal, execution of all the strokes. For instance, both the breaststroke and butterfly require the arms to be symmetrical at all times. In the rules of backstroke however, the swimmer can use one at a time or both arms together. Either method is legal as long as swimmers stay on their back.

The two-arm strategy is called the elementary backstroke. Both arms reach up and pull down simultaneously, while the legs do an inverted frog kick. The Red Cross teaches this technique for recreational as well as survival swimming. In the past it was the only way backstroke was swum in competition. Although it is considered old fashioned, it is legitimate in Masters swimming. Linda's teammate Don, who is now in his eighties, learned this method when he first started swimming and diving for the Navy, and still uses it today. Impressive to watch, he quickly and efficiently moves along, earning medals in his age group.

The "modern" way to swim backstroke uses one arm at a time with a scissors kick very similar to the freestyle, which is why it is also known as the back crawl. Linda was taught this new technique in the 1960s. In 2009, Linda learned another tip: rotation. Coach told her, "You're not a barge, you're a sleek kayak." Instead of swimming flat on her back, her shoulders lift out of the water as she raises her arms to start the stroke. Her hips follow along, rotating the whole body. She's corkscrewing through the water using the same motion taught in the freestyle. Anyway, that's the theory.

And she had to learn how to execute the new backstroke flip turn. She used to swim to the edge on her back, touching the wall with her hand before flipping over. The rules now allow a swimmer to turn onto their front when approaching the wall, make a half somersault, plant her feet and immediately push-off. Her feet now make the mandatory touch. Using less twists and turns, this proves to be a very efficient

way to turn around and was relatively easy for Linda to learn. She could envision the practicality of it. The only problem with the new turn was approximating the timing, and that's why the placement of the backstroke flags is so important. During the warm-up this morning, Linda practiced this. Once she's under the flags, she'll count three strokes to get in the proper turn position.

Linda's plan for this race is to start out comfortably, establish a rhythm and then build speed towards the end. It doesn't feel as if she's moving very fast on this first lap, so she's a bit surprised to see the backstroke flags coming into view so soon. She waits until she's under them and starts to count her arm strokes. One, two, three, and now it's time to roll over. Happily, she can see that she counted correctly. She looks down and slightly back to make sure that she has crossed over the black T bar, and it's time to flip over, touch the wall with her feet and push off.

BACKSTROKE *LAP TWO*

*Swim practices are always challenging and sometimes
require a nap afterwards.*

As she breaks the surface, she takes in a big gulp
of air. Her flip turn was successful—one down and six
to go. She tells herself to breathe deeply and regularly
and concentrate on her backstroke. Linda turns her
head slightly and sees the swimmer in the lane next
to her. With all the commotion and splashing only her
arms are visible as she strokes, following along closely. Nervous about the race, Linda had not introduced
herself before the swim, but will make an effort to congratulate her, whatever the outcome, when they both
finish.

This other swimmer moving along next to her
reminds Linda of a previous swim when Linda was
intently watching someone else's arms move right
along with hers: her sister Tracy's arms. That particular backstroke race happened a long time ago, when
Linda was a senior in college. It was the last meet of
the year, the most important one too—the New York
State Collegiate Championships.

Tracy was a freshman, studying for her ultimate career in teaching and was also going to be at the meet, swimming for a rival college. Linda the breaststroker, decided to infringe into her sister's territory and compete in the 100 yards of backstroke, Tracy's favorite event, knowing full well that they would be competing against each other. Linda made the decision anticipating a sister-to-sister show-down.

In the preliminaries, Tracy placed seventh and Linda came in eighth, which meant that they would face each other for the semi-finals. In age group swimming, college meets and the Olympics, there are preliminary trials where everyone swims. The semi-finalists are those swimmers who place 7th through 12th. The finalists are those who swim the fastest and place in the top six. At the Olympics and in larger pools, these rankings are determined by the number of lanes available. These days there are usually 8 or 10 swimmers in each heat, which means that the top 10 are finalists, and 11th place to 20th compete in the semi-finals. In Linda and Tracy's collegiate meet there were six lanes in the competition pool.

When it came time for the semi-finalists to swim, the announcement went out loud and clear, "In Lane 3, Tracy Hepworth and in Lane 4, Linda Hepworth." Now the whole meet knew that there were dueling sisters in the pool. Tracy and Linda both started out fast and swam like their reputations and their entire lives depended on this one outcome. By the fourth and final lap, they were both half the pool length ahead of the rest of the field. Linda just out-touched Tracy, securing the 7th spot. Their faster times would have placed the sisters 2nd and 3rd in the finals, but Linda had no regrets. It was the first time she had swum faster than Tracy and she felt very proud. Linda's coach just smiled and asked why she didn't swim like that all the time. It was the support of her coach and her college teammates that gave her the confidence to take on her usually faster sister.

Linda had always been a member of a supportive team both in age group swimming and in college. But when Linda got the call to join Masters swimming, she began by practicing alone in her 20-yard pool. She confidently knew what she was doing, going through her routine. She pushed herself, swimming ever in-creasing numbers of laps and eventually felt strong enough to register for a local meet.

She rose early on a Saturday morning and drove into San Francisco where the University hosts a small annual event. She recognized a few people from her neighborhood, including Sharlene, who was walking around with a clipboard. Surprised to see her friend, Linda approached and asked rather abruptly, "You coach?" Sharlene answered, "You swim?" Linda hung around Sharlene's group at the meet, listening to the advice given to each swimmer just before their event. Sharlene watched Linda swim her three races and at the end of the meet invited her to become a member of the Mud Sharks.

Linda showed up at the pool the next Monday morning. She was introduced to some of the swimmers and assigned a lane. There were very fast swimmers on this team. When Linda practiced by herself she swam about 2000 yards. This first team practice covered 3000 yards. She did keep up, barely, feeling rather slow and out of condition compared to those around her. She was bolstered by a comment from a teammate at the end of practice, "Wow! She did the whole workout!" When she saw the different techniques presented at this practice, she realized that her unchanging routine had become problematic. She wasn't going to get faster or become a better swimmer just repeating the same thing over and over again. Linda had been missing the support, camaraderie, and advice swimmers receive from an organized team. She certainly had a lot to learn.

Now she looks forward to her regular practices. Sharlene instructs her swimmers to have completed at least 600 yards as a warm up before she arrives on deck. After that, the "fun" begins. The swimmers never know what she has planned for the day—every day is different. The regimens include long distances, repetitions on a constant time interval, sprints and drills covering all the techniques. Sharlene directs her swimmers to try all four strokes, plus some fun dog paddling which helps exercise the arms for the underwater phase of the stroke. Linda's favorite non-sanctioned stroke is feet-first sculling. She's good at it and usually leads the pack. Her least favorite are the underwater laps to increase lung capacity. She has a hard time with those, as she tends to float to the surface long before reaching the end of the pool.

During the rest breaks, the swimmers catch their breath, chat a bit and catch up with news, both in the swimming world and in their personal lives. The practices are always challenging and sometimes require a nap afterwards. Under Sharlene's tutelage, she has learned new techniques, improving her times at almost every meet.

One of Linda's teammates recently confided in her that she doesn't care if the practice is hard, she's just so happy to be in the water, and Linda understood the sentiment. Maybe that is what keeps swimmers coming back. The water itself is therapeutic. During one practice, Linda started to get out of the pool mid-session. Sharlene asked if she was feeling sick. "I have errands to run and have a lot on my mind today." Sharlene then said it would do her good to finish practice, that it would settle her mind and allow her to accomplish what she needed to do, which turned out to be excellent advice. After practice, Linda calmly got everything done. Linda's teammates have all commented on how much better they feel following practice, after just being in the water.

She realizes that little has changed since she was a child. As a young person, she spent so much of her time at swim practices that she continued the thought process and dreamt of swimming at night. "Wake up." her mother called out, interrupting her dreams of racing and frolicking in the water. "It's a new day, time for breakfast and then to the water for practice."

Linda says she loves being in the water, but always dreaded undressing in the chill of the morning. That part of the sport, feeling cold before first jumping

in, was and still is difficult for her. Linda became known for circling the perimeter of the pool, slowly building up her courage while all the other kids were already completing their required warm-up laps. Oh so hesitant, she was usually the last one in the water. Even now, if her teammates see her hesitating, they playfully spray her with water. "Come on in. The water's fine!"

She finds it amusing to watch her teammates do their own dance of first entering the water. Everyone has a different technique. One gets in only up to her waist and just stands on her tippy toes for a few minutes. One does a dramatic splashy dive. Some sit on the edge and dangle their feet to acclimate to the temperature. Linda jumps in, feet first, all at once. For her, it's the most painless method. She's older now and understands that her body needs the extra lengths to warm up her muscles. In reality, the initial shock of the cool water is only momentary, nothing to dread.

She is glad she trained in the habit of regular swim practices early in life. Although it is not always fun, the ritual of practice — hard, challenging, and never boring — is the necessary price to pay for excellence.

Linda feels lucky to be on a team and have such a dedicated coach. Sharlene truly enjoys her position and can be counted on for support, advice and a discreet shoulder to cry on, if needed. Linda won't need her shoulder today, she proudly tells herself. Her own shoulders are cooperating by rotating correctly, her arms are pulling and her feet are kicking: all is well. That snaps her mind back to the present with the realization that she is not at practice, but at the Nationals. All the training and hours spent in the pool practicing culminate for this moment in time. *Swim, Linda, swim.* The backstroke flags are again overhead. One, two three, flip over, somersault, and push off.

BACKSTROKE *LAP THREE*

Water is 800 times the density of air and she is
using physical laws to move through this dense medium.

Breaking the surface and gulping air, she begins
her third lap. Her adrenalin has calmed down somewhat as she remembers the technique Sharlene taught
her as a specific method for this race. Dividing the 200
yards into four 50s is called doing a broken 200. First
she swims 50 yards, stops and notes her time from the
large clock at the end of the pool. She rests for 10 seconds, and then swims another 50, rests and repeats
that twice more, adding up all the times. Sharlene has
her add an additional 4 or 5 seconds to her cumulative
time, and said that is the time she should be shooting
for with her 200. Those extra few seconds are added
because swimming eight laps straight is a lot more tiring, therefore slower, than swimming repetitive 50s
with a rest in between.

The next time through, she has Linda swim two
50s, resting between, and then swimming the last four
laps all at once. Linda's getting the hang of the progression. Then it's time to put it all together, swim

eight laps and try to get as close as possible to the calculated time. Linda swam her 200 and was within one second of the time they had predicted. She was happy. Breaking up the race like that, made sense to Linda, but that was at practice, and now it's for real. She's on her third lap, in other words, her second fifty. *Continue with the same rhythm, and don't worry about having to speed up just yet,* Linda tells herself. *I don't want to run out of energy.*

Her mind now sifts through all the other advice given to her at practice sessions. *Keep my head straight to maintain a streamlined body position. Rotate my shoulders, mimicking the keel of a ship.* Her arms stroking rhythmically one by one are doing the job of paddles. *Remember the 3-beat kick.* Her kicking feet provide the propulsion of a motor. Some would say that paddles as well as a motor could be considered redundant, but when the object is to move as quickly as possible through the water, there's no reason to let any asset go unused:

kicking hard and pulling efficiently work together to get the job done. *Stretch and reach up, then pull down strongly with every stroke.*

She takes a big breath of air, which she can do because her face is out of the water. That's the beauty of the backstroke. Besides her steady kicking, she starts to really concentrate on her stroke. She keeps her arms as straight as possible when they fly through the air reaching up to start the *pull*, but on the underwater part of the backstroke, a bent arm with her forearm perpendicular to her body, is the best way to *push* against the water. That's a funny image, *pulling* and *pushing* against water. Can one actually push against water? It seems irrational, but that's what a swimmer does.

Normally, Linda does not concern herself with the physics associated with her chosen sport. But she can't escape the fact that water is 800 times the density of air and she is using physical laws to move through this dense medium. Scientists have been studying the physics of swimming. Linda recently attended a lecture on this, given by Dr. Rod Havriluk, Ph D.

Dr. Rod started out by saying that science used to be referenced to improve swimming times. His first graph showed a steady improvement in swimming times over the first 50 years of the sport. After the 1970s, science fell out of favor due to the East German drug controversies, and the rise of pseudo-sciences. The graph showed that Olympic swimming times have gotten faster, but at a much slower rate ever since coaches lost trust in the sports scientist. Dr. Rod is bringing science back into the fold, using a computer model named MONA to illustrate what he referred to as swimming technique misconceptions.

Then his presentation showed an image of Michael Phelps, the all-time Olympic champion doing the butterfly with the words, "Don't swim like Michael Phelps." The audience made an audible gasp. What was this man talking about? According to the Doctor, Michael Phelps puts too much vertical undulation into his stroke and any excess vertical motion works against forward propulsion.

Sharlene has taught her swimmers to swim the butterfly using vertical undulation to bring the shoulders up over the water, enabling the forward swing. Rotating her shoulders as Linda does this backstroke accomplishes the same thing, bringing her arms out of the water for a much easier swing through the air. Linda noted that the computer depiction of MONA's flat technique has her shoulders still under the water as she begins her forward stroke, making it harder to swim the butterfly. Andrew McPherson received the Pacific Masters 2017 top swimmer of the year award and understands undulation. He called butterfly the Alice in Wonderland stroke: "the hurrier you go the behinder you get," meaning the faster you turn over your stroke, the flatter you get, which slows you down.

Dr. Rod continued on to say that the glide associated with the streamline part of the stroke was not necessary. He prescribes no gliding which he said was really resting. "Do you want to rest, or do you want to swim?" Sharlene has often mentioned the glide associated with the butterfly as well as the breaststroke, making use of every forward motion produced by kicking.

There were murmurs throughout the audience of competitive swimmers, indicating that what was being said didn't seem right. Linda's friend Jack Fleming who swims for the University of San Francisco, stood up and told everyone that he swims, glides and rests and is the US Masters' World Champion in the 200 butterfly. Apparently Jack wasn't buying these controversial ideas, and he wasn't the only one.

Throughout the presentation, MONA was utilized to illustrate techniques that seemed contrary to the prevailing understanding of the sport. The computer changed the angle of the arm stroke of the butterfly, with the elbows bent behind the back in what appeared to be a very abnormal, almost insect-like position. There were many charts and graphs showing mathematical angles of the anchor/catch, elbow leverage, and a difference between the sexes when it came to the hand entry position. He suggested that a human should be able to swim 100 meters freestyle in 40 seconds, using these techniques. At this writing, the Olympic record is about 47 seconds. As a fun comparison, Linda takes about double the time, 1 minute and 20 seconds, to swim 100 meters of freestyle. Then Dr. Rod said, "Computer models are not what humans can do."

That being said, recently Linda watched a young, upcoming swimming phenomenon named Caleb Dressel break 40 seconds on his 100-yard freestyle, speeding through 4 laps with an astounding time of 39.9 seconds. That swim was in yards, and the Doctor spoke of meters, but maybe, sometime in the near future, MONA and her Doctor will have some vindication.

Linda spoke to Doctor Havriluk after the presentation and told him that it was a very interesting talk, and that it started many a conversation. He responded with a good-natured, "I didn't expect everyone to be on board." In retrospect, she regrets not asking Dr. Rod how MONA would theoretically swim the backstroke. It may have been amusing. Science and the physics of movement may play a big part in all this, but to Linda it's just swimming, as she sees the flags come into view. She'll stick to what Sharlene has taught her as she executes another successful flip turn, breaks the surface and fills her lungs with a big gulp of air.

BACKSTROKE *LAP FOUR*

That damned 11th place! It means "Close, but no cigar."

Linda opened her eyes as she was making this flip turn and through the water saw Sharlene standing at the edge of the pool timing her. She was happy that she made a good turn with Coach watching. *Let her see that I've listened to what she's told me.* She's on her fourth lap now, almost halfway there. She'll maintain her pace for the next two laps, with the intent to start to build to a sprint for the last fifty.

She thought of the Nationals in 2010, where she swam backstroke. The Masters Swimming organization had been so welcoming to the Hepworths in 2009 that Linda, Jeri and Mark decided to attend the next Summer Nationals. Georgia Tech in Atlanta, home of the 1996 Centennial Olympic Games, hosted that meet. As they finalized the plans to swim in Atlanta, Linda called an old schoolmate. Taffy was Linda's best friend from years ago in Orlando, Florida, Linda's drainage ditch buddy. She was also a water athlete but her expertise was in springboard diving, not lap swimming.

Taffy was a natural gymnast, and the twists, turns and flips necessary to perform the dives came easily to her. She was thrilled that the family was still swimming all these years later and was happy to come along. She drove down from her home in Virginia, stayed for the weekend, went to the meet and cheered everyone on, just like the old days.

When they arrived and first saw the beautiful pool, Linda noted that the diving boards were up and apparently available for use. Taffy respectfully declined the gentle ribbing, the repeated prodding that she get up there and show everyone what she could do. She quietly confided that it had been too many years with no practice. This was probably a wise decision; nobody wanted anyone to get hurt.

Atlanta was memorable—another world class competition—and Jeri, Linda and Mark each finished in the Top 10 in their respective age groups, earning coveted medals. The 200 backstroke was Linda's first race in Atlanta, the same event she's swimming now.

Jeri had signed up to swim it too and they found themselves in the same heat: a repeat of the dueling Hepworth sisters. This time they were not swimming side by side, exactly. There was a swimmer between them, who joined in the celebration of the two sisters flanking her. Mark and Taffy came down on the pool deck to closely watch the match-up.

"Take your mark." Linda pushed off at the sound of the buzzer. This was different than when Linda went head to head against Tracy so many years ago because she couldn't see Jeri, two lanes over. What she could see clearly was both Taffy and Mark urging her on as she made her turns at the 50, the 100 and the 150 yards. She had been training with the Mud Sharks team for a few months, and the lessons that Sharlene taught came to mind: *rotate your shoulders and pull your arms down strongly*. Additionally, she saw Mark making hand motions for her to increase her kicking. *Remember the importance of a good kick*.

That was a good swim, a good memory. Linda finished ahead of Jeri in that race with a very good time, just under three minutes, earning a medal for 8th place. Jeri finished in the infamous 11th place, being bumped out of a medal by her sister, and said nonchalantly, "You're significantly faster than I am in the backstroke."

After such an exhilarating swim, Linda was on a high note as she prepared for her second event: backstroke again, 50 yards. Just having placed in the top ten for the 200, and winning a medal, she knew she could easily swim the 50. What's another 2 laps? *Piece of cake*, she thought. *Up one lap and back, I've got this!* She was even dreaming about showing off two medals to her friends when she got back home, counting her chickens prematurely.

The 50 began. Linda got a good push-off and felt her backstroke rhythm fall into place. *This is a sprint,* she told herself. Her arms were wheeling around. Her feet were kicking a solid three beats per arm stroke. She felt good and strong, moving through the water as fast as she could. As she passed under the flags for the turn, she flipped over onto her front...

Uh oh, she saw right away that she was too far from the wall, already beginning her half somersault. Any hesitation or effort to take another stroke to get closer to the wall would cause her to be disqualified. When she flipped, her feet barely touched, giving her virtually no push-off. She had lost valuable time and started kicking hard to make up, but it was too late. The damage was done.

Mark was watching and later consoled her. "Too bad you missed your turn." In a thirty-second race, those few precious seconds really count. The time she lost, less than half of a second, turned out to be significant. Tenth place was 39.32 and Linda had swum 39.80, putting her in 11th place. That damned 11th place! Atlanta had given both Linda and Jeri membership in the Eleventh Place Club. It means, "Close, but no cigar."

A loss like that illustrates how important the split seconds are. At the time, she was disappointed but also knew the importance of shifting to positive thoughts.

It was no time to dwell on failure, as if 11th place at the Nationals could in any way, be considered a failure. Besides, the enthusiasm and positive vibes around her were contagious.

Remembering that mistake, she brings herself to the present: *try not to miss any of these turns*. When she was learning this new backstroke turn, it was easy for Linda to calculate the distance when she was swimming in meters. Exactly four arm strokes, once she was under the flags, got her right where she wanted to be. But in Atlanta and today, the race is in yards and that wasn't as easy to ascertain. It's shorter in length, so sometimes she counted three and sometimes four. Sharlene came to her aid again, telling her that there should be no confusion. If it's sometimes three and sometimes four, the answer is three. That settled it. *Thanks, Coach.* Now, swimming in yards she counts three strokes, kicking extra hard to make up the little bit of extra distance.

Before she learned this valuable lesson of how many strokes to take and make a definitive decision, there were a number of mishaps during practice where Linda hit her head on the wall of the pool. Thankfully no harm was done, her cushioned cap protected her. Or maybe it was because she just wasn't going very fast. She said at the time that she had miscounted her strokes, but perhaps she was daydreaming, watching the birds and the cloud formations as she likes to do and did not notice the flags. She also blamed the glaring sun for obscuring her vision. Sharlene told her to take the sun into consideration during practice because for some reason, backstroke events at meets are often held at high noon with the sun overhead, and it's best to prepare for such things. At least those bumps on her head were easier to explain than the earlier mishap of swimming into the wall going forward, doing freestyle.

At a recent local meet, Linda was watching a woman swim the 50-yard backstroke. She didn't miss her turn; she did an extra one! Instead of touching the wall for a finish after 2 laps, the woman did another flip turn and started out again. It has happened to the best of us; maybe she thought the race was a hundred, which is 4 laps. There are provisions for that mistake, and the officials dropped a rope across the pool, stopping her. She looked around and smiled, realizing right away what had happened. The drop rope is used if there is a false start or other reason to stop the swimmers. The volunteer timers had recorded the woman's time when she flipped over, but it was a few milliseconds slower than if she had just touched. Her explanation was that she was so intent in doing her backstroke turns well, that she did another one. Linda thought that was cute, and there was no disqualification.

Linda recently heard the Olympic Gold Medalist Matt Grevers speak about his amazing swimming career. He was talking about his signature, winning backstroke turn and someone in the audience asked him how many strokes he takes before he flips over.

He told the crowd that as he passes under the flags, he counts two strokes before initiating his turn. Only two strokes, and that's in meters, too! Wow, he must swim fast and strong with each stroke! Linda was impressed, as she counts three strokes to make her next turn. Here's the wall again. *Count correctly and kick hard, Linda.*

BACKSTROKE *LAP FIVE*

He wasn't just a swimmer, he was a showman!

In a 200-yard race, Lap 5 is the hardest for Linda. She's already exerted herself for 100 yards and number 5 is only the beginning of the next 100. As she's thinking of the many errors she can make missing turns, or miscounting laps, she gets a mouthful of water. She fights the urge to cough and gulps for air. This has happened to her at practice before so she doesn't panic. She swallows and takes in a few deep breaths and tastes chlorine. Some of the water enters her sinuses, causing a slight ache which takes about half a lap to go away. She knows that sinus pressure very well. It's a familiar, swimmer's pain.

Of course that little problem of water in her mouth had to happen on Lap 5. Fortunately it wasn't too bad and she recovered easily. Once she finishes this lap, 6 and 7 will seem easier, and the 8th one is her favorite, because it's the last! Hopefully, she'll count her laps correctly. Although she's been somewhat lost in thought, she has been counting her laps. It's up to her to be mindful of where she is in this race today since there are no poolside counters on these middle distance events.

Unfortunate counting errors happen. One of her teammates made his final touch at the end of two laps of breaststroke, out of breath with the exertion of a 50, only to be told that he was in a 100-yard race and had to do two more. "Keep going. Two more. Two more!" everyone called out. Linda felt complete sympathy for him. She knew how tired she feels after sprinting. It's hard to repeat another sprint, just like that. Taking a deep breath he enthusiastically swam two more laps. Welcome to the sport of competitive swimming.

With that in mind, she continues on. She's rotating her shoulders, trying to push down strongly with each arm pull and keep her head straight. Her stroke falls into a familiar pattern. She decides to change thought processes from the negative to the positive and thinks about some inspirational swims she saw while she was in Atlanta.

Linda spotted a woman in a wheelchair, noticed her all four days of the meet and assumed she was a family member of a swimmer, there to show support. After Linda had finished her events, she was wandering around watching the other races. She saw the woman again and decided to talk to her. Linda thought she would be funny and ask the woman how many events she was there for, expecting a laugh as a response. Instead the woman confidently answered that she had already swum five and was about to swim her sixth!

Doris Russell at that time was 90 years old. It sure was a good thing that she did not know the motivation behind Linda's question. Linda stood a while, deciding to watch how this lady who had trouble walking could possibly swim in the National Championship meet.

One of the positive aspects of Masters Swimming is the attempt to accommodate almost everybody's enjoyment of this sport. A special chair lift is used for occasions such as this. When it came time for Doris to swim, she lifted herself from her wheelchair onto the chair lift, which lowered her into the water. The starter buzzer sounded, and she pushed off the wall with the rest of her heat. Linda then noticed all the ribbons attached to the back of Doris' wheelchair. There were many, and most of them were blue, signifying First Place. Sure enough, Doris won this event too, and added another gold medal to her collection. *What an amazing woman,* Linda thought. She had trouble maneuvering on dry land, but nobody could stop her once she hit the water.

Also in Atlanta, Linda was sitting in the grandstands with Mark as the 500-yard freestyle began. She saw on the program that this particular race was going to be swum by older men, and noted their posted times were about 15 to 20 minutes. Thinking that it was going to be a bit boring to watch them do the 20 required laps, Linda suggested they take this time to get some refreshments, a sandwich and some hot tea.

Her brother said no, she should sit right where she was, and that she would want to watch this one. He was right.

The race began and Mark told her to keep her eye on John Taylor, age 89, swimming in lane number 1. He was from Georgia and was on his home turf. When the announcer mentioned his name, there was a loud, appreciative greeting from the audience. Obviously, he was one of the local favorites. As she watched, he slowly swam each lap, almost lazily, doing a combination of sidestroke, breaststroke and freestyle. Linda smiled to herself, noting that there was no feet-first sculling, Linda's favorite, in his repertoire. This is all legal as the freestyle events allow the swimmer to choose their stroke. At each turn, he stopped to wave at the spectators, who cheered him on and waved back. He wasn't just a swimmer, Linda thought, he was a showman! She was getting into the spirit of it all, adding to the cheers each time John stopped to make his turns, acknowledging the crowd. This was exciting! John was making it fun for everybody.

After he completed 18 laps, he thoroughly surprised Linda by streamlining his body, pushing off with vigor and sprinting with perfect form and much speed for the last two laps. The crowd was on its feet. The cheering was deafening. It was wonderful. John came in 5th in that race. Amazingly, there were four other men, ages ranging from 85 to 87, all swimming a little faster. Linda's spirits are buoyed by remembering the fine spectacle of a swim put on by John Taylor. She thinks if he can do it, she certainly can do it, and starts kicking with extra vigor, just like John.

Linda's at the wall again. The dreaded lap 5 is over! Linda executes another flip turn, noting she has only three more laps to go.

BACKSTROKE *LAP SIX*

Daydreaming got her through her long 500
and is with her again through the backstroke.

Her mind again drifts back to Atlanta. During the down time between swims, Linda and Taffy reminisced about all the fun they had together with their adventures and mishaps. Taffy at one time had lived in the Decatur area, right outside of Atlanta and drove Linda around to see her old home. They went out to lunch and ate a hearty steak meal served with the favorite Southern side dish, grits. Linda wanted the extra protein and sustenance for her upcoming events.

Out of the blue, Taffy asked her if she remembered the time they pooped in the lake. Linda was taken aback. She certainly knows better than to do anything like that! Then it all came back to her. It was summertime in Florida, hot and humid. The only respite from the heat was in the lake. Linda's mother saw the kids only occasionally when they came into the house for meals or to use the bathroom. That particular day the girls were reluctant to leave the water, even though nature was calling. It may have been on a bet or a dare, as the two girls challenged each other whenever they could. What happened to the result? Did it drop to the bottom? Did something eat it? What about the fish and snake poop? Oh, the questions they had; all scientific inquiries, of course.

A similar occurrence, years ago in the lake in New York, was not deliberate. She was waterskiing, took a tumble and water rushed up her butt. Linda got an involuntary enema. She was sore from the fall and had strange bruises to show for it later. She was very embarrassed and never said a word. Only God, the lake and she knew what had really happened. She did not water ski for a while after that. Linda now understands and heeds the signs along the shoreline: DO NOT DRINK THE WATER.

The two friends went back to the pool just in time to watch Mark swim. Uncharacteristically, he seemed extra nervous and concerned about his up-coming event, the infamous 200-yard butterfly. Mark is usually positive and prides himself on his abilities. He's tried to get his friends, and even his sisters, to attempt the very difficult event along with him. Since he appeared to be experiencing a rare lapse of confidence, Linda, Jeri and Taffy all gave him a pep talk and a back rub. While the back rub may not have alleviated his fears, he said we were his favorite sisters, at that moment.

Soon his heat was up, he was on the blocks, and the whistle blew. Linda watched as his legs kicked strongly and his arms reached and pulled for eight long lengths of the pool. Linda felt for him. She had just finished her 200 backstroke, which comes relatively easy to her, but it can be a grueling event, and needs to be swum with a strategy. Butterfly is something else. She can't even fathom attempting such a race.

Her brother Mark is a strong swimmer. He told Linda about a practice session where his coach gave the team a difficult regime. They were to swim ten 100s on a tight interval with not much rest between each. That's almost like sprinting a 1,000-yard event. Mark was swimming with younger men on his team—and keeping up. When they finished, Mark's coach gave him a little ribbing, saying that he must be tired. Linda asked, "What did you say to him?" Mark answered, "I didn't say anything. I turned around and swam a 200 butterfly!" His teammates think he's a little crazy.

Linda was thinking about that, and the amount of stamina it required while she watched her brother swim. Huffing, puffing and breathing hard, Mark successfully finished with a noticeable sigh of relief. His time was 2 minutes and 32 seconds. That put him in 10th place, earning a well deserved medal for 200 yards of butterfly "that very few people can do."

Jeri, the freestyler, won five medals in Atlanta. She came in 4th for her 1,000-yard event, 9th in the 200 free, and 10th place each for her 500, 100 and

50-yard races. The only freestyle event she did not swim was the 1650. Because of pool availability and time concerns, swimmers could enter either the 1,000 or the 1,650, but not both. So Jeri had swum, and conquered, every free-

style event that she could. The 200 backstroke, swimming against Linda, was her 6th event and the only one that she did not place in the top ten. Her perfect record of a medal in each swim was foiled by her sister. A good sport, she escorted both Linda and Mark to collect their hard earned medals. Since Jeri won so many, she knew just where to go. The Atlanta meet of 2010 was a very successful outing. But that was years ago. In this sport, you can't rest on your previous laurels. Like the investment firms advertise, "Previous performance is no guarantee of future results."

Counting her family's return to the sport in 2009 and the trip to Atlanta, today marks Linda's third appearance at a Masters Nationals. She's in Santa Clara, California at the George F. Haines International Swim Center, a beautiful, state of the art facility. It is the home of many champions including Mark Spitz and Donna DeVarona, names Linda recalls from the 1970s. They and many other Olympic champions since, all swam here under Haines' legendary tutelage. He groomed so many swimmers to achieve their dreams that the entire swim complex is named for him. A bronze statue of George, holding his ever-present stopwatch, keeps an eye on the festivities.

This year is an even bigger competition than in 2009 or in 2010. She asked an official and was told that over 2,000 swimmers were registered this year. Sharlene told her to expect the competition today to be deep, meaning many fast swimmers in each category. Linda will have time to watch some of the races after she's finished.

Daydreaming got her through a long 500 this morning and is again with her through these laps of backstroke. She is not the only one to use this technique of keeping her mind busy as she swims. Linda read about the French swimmer Benoit (Ben) Lecomte as he prepared for his historic swim across the Pacific. Now that's a LONG swim—taking 6 months to go from Japan to San Francisco. He told the media that he had his thoughts all planned out, what he would think about each day during the long, lonely hours in the water.

He was attempting this amazing feat to bring the world's attention to the pollution of our oceans. His itinerary included circumventing the huge mass of plastic that has accumulated, due to our bad habits. Even though he had to abort his swim because of bad weather, Lacomte raised an important issue. Linda always talks about the pleasure of swimming in clean waters and she wants that for the whole world. She silently apologizes as she remembers the unhealthy blunder she made as a kid. Now that's worth thinking about as she sets her mind to finishing this 200 back-stroke. One lap at a time, she's getting through this. Deep breath, turn over, somersault and push off.

"Who in their right mind would be here so early in the cold morning,
lugging 30 pounds of gear, if they weren't a swimmer?"

Linda pushed off the wall, facing up. *Lap 7—the last fifty yards, only two more laps to go.* She hears her coach's voice telling her to start building her race, in other words, slowly increase her speed with the intention of sprinting to the end. To do that, she uses her feet to kick harder and her core to use more of her whole body in pushing back the water. Her arms are not moving noticeably faster. Some swimmers flail, in other words swing their arms rapidly. Linda has always used a slower, methodical, turn-over rate. One of her teammates observed that she has an efficient stroke, moving a lot of water with each arm pull, but suggested that she do it faster.

Linda hears another voice from her grandmother all those years ago, saying she has a very pretty stroke but needs to speed up! But if Linda does that, it breaks her form. The flailing that Linda sees with competitive swimmers comes from the attempt to move as fast as possible, to get to the wall first, at all costs. It's reminiscent of the tale of the tortoise and the hare. The hare is "flailing" using a lot of extraneous energy, and ultimately loses to the tortoise using a more consistent and steady process.

Linda ponders the fact that she never had that drive, that competitive instinct, the need to place first. Champions have that as a priority and are probably not following Linda's example of dreaming their way through their races. Linda has always admired faster swimmers, the persistence and hard work that's required to accomplish their goals. She's repeatedly watched films of champions Michael Phelps, Katie Ledecky and Missy Franklin and come away with deep respect for their talents.

Linda's teammate Mary told her that ever since she was a young swimmer, she envisioned each race before she swam it. Concentrating completely, she knew how many strokes she would take and at what intervals she was going to breathe. Mary is a champion. Linda's sister Tracy also has that drive. When she swims, she swims to win. Her stroke is all power, and her many medals and first place showings attest to her determination.

A few years ago, after swimming the backstroke at a local championship meet, Linda checked the posted results, but could not find her name. *Maybe I got disqualified!* She thought back, replaying her start and all her turns, trying to recall if she had committed any grave errors. After a few seconds of worry, she checked the posting again and gasped. Not only had she not gotten disqualified, she had won first place! First place! Overcome with pride and excitement, she then understood the allure of winning.

Linda returned to her team's tent with the news that she had won her event. She had to admit that coming in first felt great! She told them of the emotional roller coaster she had just experienced of not seeing her name, including the possibility of a disqualification. Ever the comedienne, she made her teammates laugh when she explained that she just wasn't used to finding her name at the top of the list.

She remembers another backstroke race that she won, but almost did not get to swim. The meet was at the University of San Francisco, early on a Saturday morning. She had arranged to car-pool with three of her teammates. They had all been to this particular venue before and knew that parking was an issue, so it was much better to go in one car, and not take up four parking spaces. They arrived half an hour early, easily finding parking right near the entrance. They smiled to each other noting that they were almost the first ones to arrive. It was foggy and cold on top of one of San Francisco's famous hills, so the teammates stayed in the warm car until the doors opened, watching all the other swimmers arrive and start to line up at the aquatic center. Soon there was a murmur through the crowd, something about a waiver and an ID required. Linda wasn't worried about the liability waiver. She had electronically checked that box on the registration form, as she does for every meet. But her identification was another matter.

Even though, the forms tell the swimmers to bring their USMS card with them, Linda has never been asked to produce it, so stopped carrying the card to the meets. She didn't want to worry about losing any valuables while she was swimming and wasn't doing any driving so didn't bring her wallet. She had some money in her pocket for an emergency, but no license or ID.

One of her teammates got out of the car and brought back liability waiver forms for everyone to sign and present at the door. Apparently the University had to have the paperwork in hand. As Linda entered, she saw that all of the swimmers were producing their USMS cards, and a drivers' license. *Uh oh.* She had neither. Her teammates promised they would vouch for her.

The young students volunteering at the door did not know what to do with the ID-less Linda. There was a hold-up in the line, which made everyone behind her a bit testy. Linda spoke quietly to her teammates. If worse came to worse she would just watch the meet, or maybe volunteer as a timer. That could be fun. In her mind, that thought, to be just a spectator and not a participant was almost a relief. Her irrational pre-swim jitters were doing the talking. But then Linda's rational mind took over and she spoke up: "Who in their right mind would be standing here, so early in the morning, in the cold, lugging 30 pounds of gear if they weren't a swimmer?" The gate opened, Linda went through, and the line started to move again; a crisis averted.

Once inside, she found the registration desk and was relieved to see that her name was listed. As always at these meets, she acknowledged her presence by initialing near her name and circling both the 50 and the 100 backstroke events. She had plenty of time before her first event, the 50-yard backstroke. She found some space in the women's locker room to store her backpack and proceeded to get ready. With her suit and cap on and her goggles affixed, she got in the water and swam her warm-up laps. She turned onto her back, and felt good. She knew right away that it was a good day for back-stroke. After all the drama at the door, she felt happy to be in the water and not up in the grandstands with the spectators. This is where she was supposed to be.

Something else happened at that meet that made Linda feel special. She did well in her two events, placing second

in her 50 and first in her 100. But it wasn't the ribbons, or the fact that she swam fast times that made
those swims memorable; it was the reaction of her fellow swimmers. Linda got out of the water after winning her 100 backstroke to see two swimmers watching her. They asked what her time was. When she said
"1:25.07" they used the word "amazing" to describe
her swim. Linda smiled and thanked them. She has
watched and admired faster swimmers and now someone was doing that to her. *That was amazing!*

Linda really starts to swim hard now. She's going
into her last flip turn and readies herself to sprint this
last lap. Deep breath, turn over, somersault and push
off.

BACKSTROKE *LAP EIGHT*

She makes a final touch, thankfully with no extra drama.

She breaks the surface for the last time. Linda is now reaching, pulling and kicking as hard as she can, calling on all her reserved energy to finish. She can hear herself breathing extra hard now, gulping as much air as possible. Her ears are underwater, listening to the same sounds as if she's breathing in a space suit. It reminds her of one of her favorite songs by The Moody Blues entitled *Progression*. Linda does not give herself permission to start singing!

Linda lost track of the swimmer in the next lane long ago. Presumably, she is well ahead. If she were behind, Linda would be able to see her arms. But the only arms that are visible are her own as they swing past her field of view over her head, straining and lengthening. Gone are the relaxing thoughts of past swims and yesterdays. The sky is a cloudless blue—no markings on which to concentrate. Nothing to think about except, keep moving as quickly as you can. Linda's full concentration is on trying to finish this last lap. *This is amazingly hard work.* Very tired, her arms are complaining. *Keep going. Keep going. Where are those flags?* Finally, she catches a glimpse of the flags' shadow. It's only their shadow and she still has a few strokes to get under them. Thankfully, this lap goes faster than the others, or so it seems as the backstroke flags now for the last time, are overhead. Start to count. This time she will count to four to get as close as possible to the wall for her finish.

Oh no! A bad memory emerges. She's remembering when she hit her head at a meet coming in for a touch in backstroke during a 100 Individual Medley. Mark had told her to be very quick turning from the backstroke to the breaststroke, "It's OK to swim right into the wall." Linda's not sure why she decided to listen to that advice. The race was in a 50-meter pool, divided into two 25 yard pools by a large bulkhead. Coming to the wall with her backstroke, she literally swam right into the hollow bulkhead, making a loud, reverberating sound with her head. Her outstretched arm was pushed up at a strange angle. A few seconds passed as she got her bearings and turned around. It was an awkward transition, and apparently, noisy.

The freestyle flip turn, the backstroke turn and two-handed turns required for both breaststroke and butterfly were easy for Linda to learn. The turn going from the backstroke to the breaststroke in the individual medley is another thing. Most swimmers use an open turn for this, but Linda has recently noticed the younger, faster swimmers using a new flip here. They turn on their front and somersault like making a back-stroke flip-turn, but coming off the wall they have to be on their front for the breaststroke pull-down. This is tricky and involves an extra twist in there somewhere, so Linda uses the old fashioned method of swimming to the wall on her back, hopefully touching it with her hand and not her head! She then brings her legs up and pushes off on her front. It's probably slower, but better than being disqualified by being in the wrong position off the wall.

After she bumped her head and got herself turned around, she swam a lap of breaststroke. She made certain that she touched the wall with two hands and started back with her last lap of freestyle. When she finished and looked up, there were three officials con-gregated at her lane, calling out her name and asking if she was all right. Apparently everyone at the meet knew she had "swum right into the wall."

To ensure that she won't do that today, she reach-es out, extending her shoulder as far as she can. She kicks her last strong kick and makes a final touch, thankfully with no extra drama. And she's done! *Eight laps of backstroke. Phew!*

Taking off her dark goggles, she looks around. One woman on the other side of the pool was just finishing. She didn't come in first, but at least she wasn't the very last one in her heat! She ducks under the water a few times to cool her face. Her time is listed on the scoreboard, but Linda's eyes are blurry from the goggles and she can't read it clearly. She'll find out soon enough. The bright light of the day shimmers over the surface of the pool, now calm, as the water readies itself for another race. Linda smiles at her coach, her family and some of her teammates who cheered for all eight laps. With her heart pumping strongly, she uses the ladder to pull herself out of the pool.

Participating in these swimming competitions is certainly cardio-intensive. Linda's heart starts beating strongly in her chest right as she gets in line for her heat, even before she begins her deep breathing exercises. Her body anticipates the effort. Her pulse is still quick and strong, only now starting to slow up a bit as she heads to the warm-down pool for a few very leisurely laps to help ease her body back from a high alert stage. The meet is moving right along as the whistle blows for the next heat of women to step up to the blocks for their swim.

After eight relaxing laps, Linda gets out of the water, finds her towel behind the timers and walks to her family. Greeted like a triumphant war hero returning home, she receives lots of congratulations, slaps on the back, and high fives. They all understand her feelings of happiness and success. Sharlene shows Linda her splits, how fast she was going on each leg of the 200. She's coached Linda to start out slowly in these middle distance races, set a tempo and then "build speed" as she feels comfortable. Linda did not heed that advice. Her last laps were slower than her first. In Linda's case, the theory of using practiced strategies only sometimes becomes reality. When she began this race, she had reminded herself of her plan. She knows how to swim the 200, but was too tired to speed up when she was supposed to. Concentrating on reliving her swimming life and daydreaming of other races, she had not started out slowly enough to have any reserved energy. Her final time of 3:07 placed her 12th in her age group. At least it wasn't 11th place.

EIGHT

Did she really admit to her coach that a butterfly event was fun?

Now that she's well into the day, her nerves have settled down. Relieved that two of her hardest events are over, Linda can relax a bit. She still has the 200 breaststroke to swim and the upcoming relay with her sister, and she's looking forward to both of those. And then she will finish with her 50-yard backstroke.

She could be wrong, but she's thinking that the 50 back will be a piece of cake, a lot easier than these 200s, but she has to keep a focused mind until she's completely finished. Her conscience reminds her that her cavalier attitude about a 50-yard backstroke race, with a missed flip turn, caused her to miss out on a medal at the last Nationals. *Keep focused and you can do it,* Linda says to herself. Regardless of the race length, a strategy still needs to be followed to ensure she swims well. Complacency will work against her. She'll think about that later. Right now Linda has time to spend with her family, sit in the grandstands and watch some of the races. Coach Sharlene has said that a swimming meet can be boring for a spectator but Linda doesn't share that opinion. She loves to watch the competition at the meets and any time swimming is televised. Each event has the opportunity to showcase the thrill of victory as well as the agony of defeat.

Linda turns her attention to the announcers. They keep the spectators informed and entertained. One in particular, Dave Wierdsma, does such a good job at her local meets that Linda looks forward to hearing his voice. He uses stories, quips and an excellent sense of humor to keep the meets interesting. And if any race ends in disappointment, he speaks in a sympathetic tone. Dave earned the Peggy Lucchessi Award for "exemplifying the joy and spirit of Masters Swimming" in 2017.

The announcer acts as the MC of the meet, informing everyone of what event is in the pool and what's coming up. "This is heat number 2 of the men's 400 freestyle, just coming to an end. Heat number 3: get ready. You're up next." Linda likes it when they point out specific swimmers: "Lane 6 is the one to watch in this race, as Laura Val attempts to better her own world record in the 100-meter backstroke." And when she did, everyone applauded. Recently at the Northern California Long Course Championships, Linda watched Laura break three world records in one day. Later, walking towards the locker room, Linda caught up to her and asked if breaking all those records ever gets old. Laura just smiled.

At some meets, if time allows, each swimmer is identified. Lane 1 through 8, the announcer gives the name, the club affiliation and any interesting fact: first time competing, or returning from an injury. The announcers get the crowd excited with ongoing commentary when the races are especially close. And they usually announce the winner of each heat. Linda heard her name once when she was finishing a 100-meter breaststroke event. She was winning her heat, out in front. Too busy trying to finish well, she couldn't wave or otherwise acknowledge the honor, but she heard it!

Recently Linda told a friend that she had just spent the day at a swimming meet, but there was nothing interesting to report. Then Linda finished the sentence with the word except. There was nothing interesting to report except she had watched Laura Val break all those records. A man fully recovered from cancer and chemotherapy swam like a champ. Linda saw a woman take off her prosthetic leg and swim butterfly. Courageous and inspirational!

At that particular meet, a coach from another team actually stopped (and got disqualified) in the middle of the 100 butterfly. No harm was done. Apparently he had gotten a cramp. He was ready to go a few hours later in his other events.

And for something new at that meet, Linda swam the butterfly leg of her team's relay: 50 meters in a long course pool, one very long lap with no turns. It was only the second time Linda swam butterfly as an adult in competition. She did surprisingly well. Instead of tiring in the middle, she felt her energy surge, taking 2 seconds off her previous time. It was exhilarating and she even told Sharlene that it was fun. So it was not an "uneventful" swimming meet after all. Linda pauses to think here. Did she really admit to her coach that a butterfly event was fun? The excitement of swimming well must have clouded her brain! Sharlene acknowledged that she should never have told her that. She'll expect Linda to be doing the butterfly from now on!

At the next meet, with excitement and nervousness, Linda asked if she was slated to swim the butterfly leg of the relay. Sharlene very diplomatically acknowledged that Linda's butterfly time was 44 seconds. Yes, yes, nodded Linda with pride. Then Sharlene continued, "Your teammate Martha swims it in 36 seconds." *Oh...so, Martha will be doing the butterfly.* That made sense to Linda; she could not argue with an eight second difference. The point in all of this is to enter the fastest swimmers, especially in a relay. Linda led off with her signature backstroke, Martha did the butterfly, and they won a medal! Linda has gone on to swim the 50 butterfly in more individual events, and has now improved her time to 40 seconds but still has a long way to go to catch up to Martha.

NINE

~~~~~~

200-YARD BREASTSTROKE

Keep your head low and glide long.

Before she knows it, it's time for Linda's third event of the day, the 200-yard breaststroke. This stroke brings to mind leisurely swims in a pool or a lake, head out of the water looking around enjoying the environs, arms under the water gently pushing the water back and legs kicking like a frog, gliding, gliding through the water. Racing in this format, however, is another story.

Swimming eight laps of breaststroke requires a lot of stamina. It feels repetitive and tedious and can be frustrating because it's slow compared to the other strokes. During one 200, Linda's teammates were congregated at the far end of the pool, cheering her on. One well-intentioned man called out how many more laps she needed to go at each turn: Only 7 more; only 5 more... At the time she knew he was trying to be helpful but the "calling out" only seemed to reinforce what a long way she still had to swim, one slow stroke at a time.

To begin the breaststroke, she streamlines her body, with the exception of out-spread arms. She pulls back strongly, bending her elbows to bring her hands just under her chest. Then Linda arches her back, bringing her head out of the water, briefly allowing a breath of air before ducking under the water again and shooting her arms forward quickly. The whip kick happens simultaneously positioning her body for the

forward glide. That would be the glide, the resting part of the stroke that Dr. Havriluk cautioned against in his swimming science lecture. Linda's coach Sharlene often refers to the glide in breaststroke and she certainly is not talking about any resting. The glide maximizes every bit of forward momentum from the kick. Sharlene knows what she's talking about, having earned two bronze medals in the Nationals for her breaststroke races, before her career in coaching. "Keep your head low and glide long." Following that important advice, Linda will glide today.

She remembers with pride her latest 200 breast-stroke victory. She won first place using the glide, at the Northern California Short Course Meters Championships. But that was a local meet; this is Nationals—many more women in her age group, from all across the nation.

After a few deep breaths, Linda steps up on the blocks. She hears the whistle signaling the start of her event, crouches to give the extra push off, and waits for the familiar, "Take your mark." When the electronic buzzer sounds, she dives into the water.

BREASTSTROKE *LAP ONE*

Wisdom dictates for one to savor every moment,
and Linda is doing just that.

Linda enters the water, arms out-stretched in front, head tucked low, streamlining, trying to get the most distance out of her dive. Her goggles are securely on, thank goodness. *So far so good*...she has to be careful here to not repeat a mistake she made years ago with another 200-yard breaststroke race.

Her training makes it almost second nature to go on automatic pilot and follow this mental pattern when starting a race: take a deep breath, dive and immediately start kicking. Unfortunately, in that race many years ago, the "automatic" kick that her mind chose was the flutter kick. She had not envisioned her breaststroke race beforehand. She hadn't specifically told herself what event she was doing, and she started swimming the wrong stroke.

The flutter kick accompanies the freestyle, or crawl. It is illegal to do the flutter kick with the breaststroke; a cause for disqualification. She did three or four of these kicks, providing plenty of opportunity for the judges to see what could be construed as cheating on Linda's part. Quickly realizing her mistake, she did a strong whip kick and breached the surface with a legal breaststroke break-out. Unexplained luck was with Linda that day. Apparently none of the judges had noticed the illegal kicks. Perhaps the turbulence of the water as she entered obscured the officials' view. But she's watched many a swimmer dive in, and she can clearly see what they're doing. There was no explanation except that Linda was just fortunate. She felt slightly guilty about "getting away" with something and mentioned it to her mother later. Apparently Linda did not feel that guilty, as her confession came hours after the results were posted.

That happened a long time ago, but she remembers it quite clearly today. *This is breaststroke*, she tells herself, *a 200. You're doing eight laps*. She pulls her hands down through the water, executing a perfectly legal breaststroke kick, bringing her to the surface with her arms out in front of her. Pulling back with bent elbows snapping underneath her body, she then shoots her arms forward, extending into a "Y" preparing for the next stroke.

Establishing a rhythm is not only the key to be able to maintain her momentum for eight laps, it also allows her thoughts to turn to her performance at this meet. She's more than halfway through her events when she finishes this one. The day is flying by. Afternoon now, nice and warm, the sun is overhead providing perfect weather for a day at the pool.

The conditions differed this morning, when it was cool and cloudy-the air full of mist. For hours now she has watched the morning shadow being led away in a straight line across the pool, replaced by the bright light of day. Linda feels fortunate that she has already completed her 200 backstroke before the sun got so bright. Even with her dark goggles, the glare sometimes forces her to close her eyes. That's not good, as it may cause her to wander in her lane, or even worse, not see the flags and miss her turns. And because she went out a bit too fast with her 200 backstroke, she's telling herself to not make that mistake on this race. She hears Sharlene's voice telling her to make the most of every stroke: "Glide long."

The sun is casting shadows onto the bottom of the pool. Linda can see her shadow reflected, like watching a movie of her swim. Her hands are forward with fingers slightly outspread. There is a space between her arms and her ears, which is not the preferred "streamlined" position that she thought she was in. She needs to reposition a bit and work on a few things at practice—a picture is worth a thousand words. Wisdom dictates for one to savor every moment, and Linda is doing just that, with her shadow along for the ride. She's comforted by the image and she began with the right stroke, too! This race is starting with good omens. She's completed her first lap. Breathe deep, two-handed touch, turn, push-off...

BREASTSTROKE *LAP TWO*

Her love of swimming got her through college.

Beginning this next lap Linda looks down. Slightly off from her turn, she centers herself on the black line. She can see her arms pull down, keeping each hand on either side of the line as she pulls through. *Swim straight. It's the shortest distance from here to there.*

Watching her shadow reminds her of a time when she left home to go to college. She was away from her large, closely-knit family for the first time, and felt alone. She took a lot of walks on her Western New York Campus, just getting to know the place and meeting new people. On a quiet night in the dormitory, Linda drew a picture of herself. Not exactly a portrait, just her shadow as it appeared during her long walks. She drew it to remind herself of this time in her life, of the changes she was going through. She always liked that drawing. It wouldn't win any art contests, but to her, it was significant. She hasn't seen the picture in years, but here is that image again marking yet another significant time in her life.

Going away to college is a big transition for any-one, and Linda was no different. She had selected her school not for the swimming, but for the chance to travel and see the world. They had a Junior Year Abroad Program, in partnership with the University of Leeds in England. She anticipated spending her third year in England and had that to look forward to, but meanwhile she had to find her way in a new environment. Her love of swimming gave her a good starting point to find some like-minded friends on her new campus.

When she arrived at the aquatic center, she was surprised to discover that she had options, different ways she could compete in the water. She joined the fa-miliar competitive racing team right away and went to practices faithfully, keeping in mind the other aquatic sports available to her. Her college had a water polo program: playing soccer in the water. *Why not?* She tried out for it and found it fun to play until she saw how rough it could be. She was caught on the losing end of an opposing player who seemed determined to drown her. *Enough of that!*

The school also offered a synchronized swimming team, an artful, choreographed way to "dance in the water," swimming either alone or in groups. The culmi-nation of all the practices of this sport was not a meet, but a professional two-hour show. For the event, the pool area was transformed into an underwater scene, lit by blue floodlights, with a large mural of mermaids.

Linda enjoyed watching the show her first year, re-membering her dream of being a mermaid floating in her aunt's pool. Thinking she could be good at this new sport, she joined the synchronized team for her sophomore year, as well as maintaining her competi-tive racing regime.

Linda was in the water a lot. Her roommates didn't mind. There were four women living in one dorm room, using one bathroom and one shower. Linda showered and washed the chlorine out of her hair at the aquatic center every day, so that was one less person competing for time in the small dormitory bathroom. Any group or family understands that benefit.

Synchronized swimming was very different than the racing she was used to. She had to learn differ-ent movements and positions like doing ballet, but in water. Acrobatics were also included. She learned to

do tuck and layout somersaults in the water, forward and backwards. Her routines included holding herself vertically underwater, but upside down. This position was like treading water, but instead of kicking to remain afloat, she used her arms to do the work while keeping her legs perfectly upright. She used nose plugs for this, as gravity still works under the water, and she couldn't breathe out enough air to keep the water from entering her sinuses. From this inverted position, she could make geometric patterns by crossing and uncrossing her legs, connecting with the other swimmers. This looked very dramatic from above the water, which was the spectator's point of view.

Another routine required all the swimmers to line up along the edge of the pool. In perfect time with the music, they dove in, one by one just like a dance line at Radio City Music Hall. Clad in matching bathing suits with decorated caps, it was impressive to see. Linda managed to make her dive in perfect tempo to maintain the effect. Besides the line-up, she had three small roles to play, or swim, in the program.

There were older swimmers who had been practicing this sport for a long time and were doing solo numbers, each perfectly suited to the selected music. The performances were beautiful and very well received. Linda performed with the team only once because the next year she left for England. By the time she returned as a senior, the synchronized swimming team had changed. Gone were the familiar faces whose expertise she had studied and admired. She was glad she participated and admires it today. Synchronized swimming is now a sanctioned Olympic event. However, given the choice of the two water sports, racing remains her passion.

Linda's sister Jeri found that synchronized swimming was the only aquatic sport open to women when she was an undergrad. Their brother Mark attended college with the help of a swimming scholarship and competed on the collegiate level. Jeri was fast enough, but there were no women's competitive swimming teams, therefore no scholarships. She wanted to do something with aquatics, so she joined the synchronized swimming team and performed with them. When the sisters get together informally in the water, they still run through the routines they learned in synchronized swimming.

Jeri was interviewed by *Swimmer* magazine in 2010 (Sept.-Oct.). In the article she recalls that before 1972, the competitive racing team was not open to women swimmers like herself, even at the University of Florida, a state where the sport is very popular. Just before Linda started college, legislation was enacted, Title IX, granting equal access regardless of sex, to all educational programs. Title IX did not originally mention sports specifically, but instigated a lot of changes for high school as well as collegiate athletics, including competitive swimming. The law allowed the establishment of women's swim teams. Linda had taken it for granted that she could continue her competitive swimming in college, not realizing how lucky she was to have so many choices regarding the aquatic sports.

Prominent US Masters swimmers Laura Val and Christie Ciraulo were affected by the change as well, and are on record discussing their experiences with pre-Title IX restrictions. Both women were swimming at the top of their age levels through high school but could not continue on to represent their chosen colleges. As a result, Christie put her swimming on hold for 25 years, while Laura continued on with private swim clubs, although not satisfied with the level of competition, according to *Swimmer* magazine. Title IX changed all that, and now women competing in collegiate sports have become just as current and competitive as the men, giving both sexes an outlet to show off their talents.

Here's the wall again. Linda makes a legal two-handed touch, turns around, and pushes off to continue on her journey.

BREASTSTROKE *LAP THREE*

Remembering these college swimming days is a pleasant distraction.

She pulls down with a strong kick and then breaches the surface to start this next lap and continue with her thoughts of college days. Initially, Linda was surprised to find out that she was one of the fastest women swimmers on the roster; she wasn't used to that. She had come from a team loaded with extremely good swimmers, future Olympians, as well as her faster sisters. She became a leader of sorts, someone that the other swimmers looked up to. She got the nickname of *Queenie*, but never did find out what that meant exactly. Maybe it was because Linda was a bit adventurous, you might say mischievous, and the other swimmers thought she could get away with more antics just because she was a good swimmer.

One of the nice perks of being on the college team was that Linda got to travel. The meets were held in different parts of the state, and the college paid for overnight accommodations when necessary. During these weekend excursions, Linda was acquiring a reputation as the one to play practical jokes, especially on their coach Ms. Carmichael.

She remembered a particular meet when they were caught in a heavy snowstorm and had to spend an extra night at a motel. After dinner at a nearby diner, the team could not find the coach in her room. The girls went on a hunt and finally discovered her at the bar next door, obviously a bit tipsy. Perched on the lap of a new male acquaintance, her legs and feet sort of danced in the air. This was shocking, but quite funny to the team, who had never before seen the coach in such a compromised position.

Apparently Coach C had been drinking Rusty Nails. The swimmers were all underage; most had never heard of a Rusty Nail. Linda now knows what they are — a delicious combination of scotch and Drambuie over ice. Three or four of them apparently provide a perfect alternative to spending twelve hours in a small motel room with a group of 18-year-olds.

Even though the swimmers were young and did not have a vast experience with alcohol, they understood that someone might be under the weather the next morning after such a scotch-fueled evening. When morning arrived, the sun came out. It melted some of the snow, and the roads were cleared for the bus to carry the team back to their campus. Not surprisingly, the coach was sleeping later than usual.

Linda decided to use this opportunity to play a very funny trick. She told the early-rising girls to gather as much snow as they could and pile it up in front of the coach's door. They then called her room, waking her with the explanation that it had snowed even more during the night and they were stuck inside for another day due to the 6-foot drifts that had accumulated against the motel doors.

Of course Coach rushed to the door, pulled it open only to find a thick wall of snow. The loud hysterical laughter as well as the streaming sunlight through the adjoining window told the coach that she had been had! She was a good sport, though. In retrospect she probably did not feel like making much of a fuss, or scolding her girls. In fact, she seemed rather subdued on the ride home.

At another weekend meet, the team stayed in a residential hall of one of Western Pennsylvania's oldest colleges. It was a large, three-story stone building, old fashioned in style with long corridors. The set-up was for two or three swimmers in each dorm room with a communal bathroom at the end of the hall. The quaint place called out for exploration.

Halfway down the hallway was a prominent metal cabinet that housed the fuses for all the rooms, each carefully numbered. Linda thought it might be entertaining to shut off some of the fuses, but really hilarious to shut off the fuse to Coach's room. Surrounded by teammates urging her on, she was the one to pull the switch. There was a loud cry when Coach suddenly found herself in the dark. Stepping into the well-lit corridor, she automatically pointed her finger to Linda. How did she know?

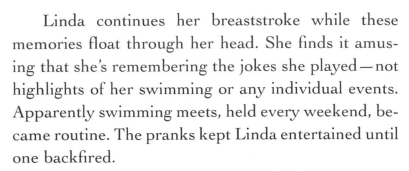

Linda continues her breaststroke while these memories float through her head. She finds it amusing that she's remembering the jokes she played—not highlights of her swimming or any individual events. Apparently swimming meets, held every weekend, became routine. The pranks kept Linda entertained until one backfired.

Coach C was uncharacteristically late for practice. The swimmers had finished their warm-up laps and were congregated in the shallow end of the pool, waiting her instructions. They happened to notice that one of the janitors had left the door open to the pool storage closet and someone, maybe it was Linda, decided to investigate. There were all sorts of fun things stored away: oars and life jackets for a non-existing rowboat, flotation devices, many kickboards and a full-size surfboard. A surfboard? What was that doing in there? Linda thought it was a good idea to bring that surfboard out and use it in the pool. Four or five swimmers all tried to climb aboard which was not an easy thing to accomplish. The board was slippery, difficult to mount and despite its tendency to float, became partially submerged with the weight of the entangled, laughing women. Coach suddenly arrived on deck. *Uh oh.*

A big panic ensued with most everyone jumping off the surfboard at once, trying to hide the fact that they were messing around. Linda, not being the swiftest to react, was still partially hanging on when the previously submerged board, now without its passengers, swiftly jutted up to the surface, hitting Linda in the ribs. That hurt, but Linda was not in any position to cry out or complain. She had no business having that surfboard in the pool. There was no explanation other than to admit that she had indeed instigated another little prank. Linda had only herself to blame for the now throbbing pain in her side, and she kept her mouth shut.

It turned out that the surfboard had broken two ribs. Linda did not fully understand the damage she had done to herself and swam in a meet the following weekend. It was a very dangerous thing to do. When she finally went to see a doctor, he told her that she could have easily made things much worse, including puncturing a lung. So you see, joking around in the water has consequences!

Remembering these college swimming days is a pleasant distraction. For her sophomore year, the whole team stayed on campus for the long Christmas holiday. The place seemed deserted and eerily quiet as most of the students had gone home for the month of vacation. The swimmers all stayed together in one house and practiced twice a day for 2 hours each. It was exhausting and exhilarating at the same time.

Linda remembers one of her non-swimming friends showing up at the house excited that the group was still on campus. He was looking for some fun, maybe hit a bar or two, do some dancing. Even though it was early on a Friday night, all the women were lounging on the couches and living room furniture. Not one of them even considered getting up, much less going out. Everyone was just too tired to move. After the grueling, literally hundreds of laps in the pool, no energy remained for anything else. Their partying friend seemed quite disappointed.

Linda swam with the college team for three years, missing her junior year when she went to England. Connecting like a family, this group practiced together every day. They swam, traveled, slept, played, competed, laughed and cried together. They bonded in life as well as in the water. At the end of their senior year, the swimmers were going their separate ways and their little team that had gotten so close, was about to disband. All good things must come to an end. How do you commemorate years spent in such a way? How could they properly thank Coach C for leading them through all the trials and successes of the last few years? The teammates thought and thought and finally came up with a symbol of strength, unity and longevity. They "pooled" their money and bought their coach a young tree, a magnificent blue spruce to be exact. She had recently purchased a new home and had the perfect place for such a gift.

Now for the presentation, the team wanted to make it special, perhaps including some fanfare leading up to it. At the last dinner/going away party the tree was still in its 10-gallon pail, hidden behind a door. Coach Carmichael arrived at the party and for some reason went straight to the back room, opened up the door, and asked, "Whose tree is that?" Well, so much for a surprise.

Linda is not surprised now that the wall is approaching as she executes another turn.

BREASTSTROKE *LAP FOUR*

It was an impressive result, but she cannot
recommend that particular pre-swim routine

Almost halfway through this 200 breaststroke, she really should be concentrating on her race, but she thinks, *this is so monotonous*. She's glad that she has her shadow and thoughts to keep her company, lap by lap. Olympic Gold Medalist Natalie Coughlin was asked what she thinks about during her grueling long prac-

tices and swims. "In the pool, it's only you and the black line and sometime the black line starts to talk back." Apparently there is something called Black Line Fever that can become somewhat mesmerizing after long hours in the pool.

Natalie further explained that she tries to maintain presence in the water, concentrating on her technique and keeping her mind on what she is doing. She mentioned that during the big events, the Nationals and the Olympics, if she was successful, she swam the same race three times: the preliminaries, the semi-finals, and then the finals. For her, there was no boredom or monotony. Natalie saw each swim as an opportunity to assess and improve with each repetition. Linda can't imagine going through these events three times each! She thought about Katie Ledecky swimming the Olympic 800 Meter Freestyle, and having to do it three times!

Linda feels something irritating her left eye. She blinks and then blinks again. It's still there, maybe an errant lash. It's under her goggles, of course, so nothing can be done right now. She closes that eye and continues swimming, hoping the annoyance will go away. She blinks a few more times, and her eye feels better. Another near-crisis averted, Linda continues on with her breaststroke. Each stroke takes a lot of effort; she consoles herself with the fact that she's only swimming this once today. That's a huge relief! Her eye irritation cleared up, her goggles are behaving and her cap is secure. She's counting her blessings.

Best of all, she can barely feel her suit. In any swimming meet, the bathing suit is very important. Since nobody wants any 'drag' in the water, the suits have to be very tight and form-fitting, and are sometimes challenging to get on. Lots of huffing and puffing in the dressing room accompany the exercise, each person having different degrees of difficulty, some asking for a helpful pull or tug when necessary.

At one of her last meets, Linda was surrounded by many women, all getting ready, struggling to get their tight suits on. Linda's suit went on quite readily and she didn't need any help. She got dressed quickly and went out to the pool for her warm-up laps. She swam her laps comfortably and as always, decided to dive in to test out the starting blocks. As she was lined up to dive, she heard the call that the warm-up was about to end. Linda was in the first event that day, the 50-meter freestyle. She dove in, thinking about her upcoming race. Right away she discovered why her suit had gone on so easily; it had completely lost its elasticity! Unnoticed when swimming laps, but when she dove, the top part of the suit filled up with water. The result was a large drag sensation. This certainly would not bode well in a race.

Linda had to change her suit, and quickly! Thankfully she had brought a new one to the meet. She was in the third heat of the first event: 50 meters of freestyle. The 50s are sprint races, and go fast. The announcers were telling everyone to stand for the National Anthem as Linda ran back into the locker room to change. Now her body was wet making it even more difficult to get the new, really tight suit pulled on correctly. There were no other women there to help her. She heard the starting buzzer go off, signaling the first heat of her event. The voice through the loud speaker in the locker room told the second heat to line up and get ready. Linda was sweating now, pulling, uncoiling the fabric, and tugging...

OK...She got it... Her suit is on. Her heart was pumping as she ran out of the locker room and arrived at her designated lane just as Heat 2 dove in. Coach Sharlene was there, clipboard in hand, frantically looking for her. Linda whispered through her heavy breathing, "I had a wardrobe malfunction."

"Heat 3, you're up! Take your mark." Beep! Linda dove in and raced as fast as she could to the end of the 50-meter pool. Her training went into automatic over-drive. She did not prepare her mind for this sprint. She did not take time to envision her technique. She did not breathe deeply and center herself. Adrenalin alone got her through that race. When she calmed down many minutes later, she found out that she had swum her fastest time in that event, by 2 seconds!

It was an impressive result, but she cannot recommend that particular pre-swim routine. Every bit of energy she had was exerted in a very short period of time. This breaststroke race she's in now is a lot different than that frenzied 50-meter sprint. She had started out by setting her pace; a rhythm, a steady pattern she could sustain for eight laps. Pull. Kick. Shoot your arms forward. Repeat. And repeat again. Breaststroke can feel tedious because of this monotony.

This has felt like a long lap and Linda figures she still has three more strokes to go. She is reminded

of a very fast breaststroker who had so much power with every arm pull, that he used only five strokes to swim one 25-yard lap. Pulling himself so efficiently through the water, he made it look easy. At the time Linda thought, *I'm going to swim the breaststroke just like that from now on!* At practice she tried to copy the young man's stroke. She was a little disappointed that she wasn't covering nearly the same distance. *I'll keep working on this! Pull. Kick. Shoot your arms forward. Here's the wall. Two-handed touch, turn around. You're halfway through.*

BREASTSTROKE *LAP FIVE*

Everyone gasped, but only for a second as the man,
being a good sport, dove in for his designated laps.

Lap 5 brings good news and bad news. The good
news is that the first 100 yards of her race is over.
The bad news is there's still 100 yards to go, and she's
starting to feel some fatigue. After her pull down, she
emerges with a much needed deep breath. *Cough, cough!*
Linda swallowed some water, bringing her back to the
present in a most abrupt way. *Really? This is happening
as I begin Lap 5?* She breathes out hard before she can
inhale for her next stroke. She coughed again.

She's relieved that she didn't swallow too much.
Linda wonders if anyone heard her or noticed the tiny
bit of distress she was under or that she momentarily
lost her stride. She choked just when she was recalling previous mishaps, days of pulling pranks, fooling
around and not being serious. Water does have a power
of its own and perhaps is trying to tell her something.
Keep your mind on your journey, Linda. She kicks hard and
propels herself forward. Glide…good, the bad chok-
ing feeling has passed. She can now take a deep breath

and resume ducking her head and pulling down. *Get through this lap and you'll be home free. Try to think positive thoughts.* Thankfully the issue with her bathing suit at the other meet is a distant memory. Maybe because this is the dreaded Lap 5, she can't help but think back to other problems she's encountered with swim-wear.

Recently Linda and a girlfriend were in the locker room, preparing for a competition. Her friend commented that her daughter is also a swimmer and has helped her Mom suit up in the past, adding that it was a true test of love when you ask your young daughter to help maneuver a tight suit over all the bulges and wrinkles. Their suits were finally on and they started to enter the pool area. *Oh, dear,* Linda thinks, *I forgot to go to the bathroom.*

With a sigh, she heads to the stalls, taking her suit off, knowing full well that it will take another few minutes to put it back on again. At least this time, her body is still dry and she's not in a rush. This problem plagues many swimmers throughout the meet: how to go to the bathroom. As anyone knows it is not easy peeling off a wet suit, not to mention getting it back on again. Has anyone ever thought of a discreet trapdoor?

A few years ago, the very fast swimmers were wearing what were called tech suits. Tech suits were extremely tight and form-fitting made with revolutionary materials that covered the whole body from the neck down to the ankles, including long sleeves. They zipped up the back giving a slick, seal-like effect in the water. Like a wetsuit, they were definitely not easy to get into and Linda witnessed numerous swimmers asking their teammates for help. The extremely snug fit of the girdle-like garment must have been uncomfortable to wear for long periods of time because swimmers waited until the last minute, literally seconds before their races, to get zipped up. Linda learned that the tightness of the suit, although a bit restricting, helped to maintain a straight, streamlined position. It's hard to bend in a full body corset. It was also advertised that the material gave the swimmer another benefit—extra buoyancy. All this technology made for faster swims but many competitors could not afford these new suits. They were very expensive, ranging between $600 and $700. The suits have since been outlawed in competitions. Linda is not sure if it was the added advantage the suits gave, or the fact that due to the expense, they were not readily available to everyone.

Linda will always remember the suits for another reason. She and her sisters were waiting to swim their relay at the Nationals in 2009. Four swimmers in each relay, ten lanes, plus the timers and officials meant there was a large crowd gathered behind the starting blocks. Standing in front was a man wearing one of the new tech suits. Linda noticed that his suit had an obvious flaw; there was a run in it, right up the back, like Linda gets in her nylon stockings. She quietly pointed this out to her sister. "Look at that! With all the money those suits cost, you don't expect a defect like that."

Just then, the man was called up for his swim. Up on the blocks he climbed, watching as his relay teammate was determinedly swimming towards the wall, coming in for his finish. As the tech-suited man crouched for his take-off, the run in the suit, previously just a small, barely noticeable line, immediately tore completely open. An impressive ripping sound accompanied the malfunction and got everybody's attention. The man's crouched position up on the blocks gave the entire crowd behind him a clear view of the complete moon and dangly. The spectators gasped, but only for a second as the man, being a good sport, dove in for his designated laps.

Murmurs and twitters sounded throughout the crowd. A lot of people had seen what had happened. The man, now with a completely ruined suit that hid nothing, had to somehow swim his laps and get out of the water; Linda was not going to miss seeing that. She had asked for a trapdoor, but certainly not one that opened without warning!

When he finished his swim, he stayed in the water and asked for help in unzipping the suit. His relay teammates eased the situation for their friend by pulling the top half down over his bottom. The man was able to climb out of the pool with some of his dignity still intact. Most of the comments Linda heard were not about the embarrassment, but were concerns of financial loss, and a possible refund. But Linda's sister was more disturbed by what she saw, and complained repeatedly, "You made me look!"

Linda had better look now, because the wall is coming up. *Pay attention here, Linda.* She's polishing off the fifth lap of this 200, her least favorite. Maybe that's why she was remembering malfunctions and problems. Plus the little bit of coughing and the hiccup made these last two laps seem even longer. She's thankful that she's more than halfway through her event and the wall is fast approaching. She has to make sure she does a level, two-handed touch here. She can see the turn judge watching every lane very carefully. This breaststroke is not for the faint of heart, and she'd hate to do all this exertion and get disqualified.

BREASTSTROKE *LAP SIX*

She remembers that day as the only time
she got out of the water and cried.

As Linda starts her pull-down for her sixth lap,
the rhythm of her stroke lulls her into a contempla-
tive mood. She recalls a meet many years ago held in
the Long Island Sound, where she also swam breaststroke. This meet was different because she was not
swimming in a crystal clear pool. The course was
in the Long Island Sound, in open water with long
docks, buoys and ropes set out to define the borders of
the competition. The water was dark and murky, and
Linda wasn't sure she wanted to see the bottom even
if she could. But that wasn't the main issue. Jellyfish
will be the operative word here.

Jellyfish seemed to squish between her fingers as
Linda was trying to do her laps. She might not have noticed the little creatures if she were doing backstroke,
or a very fast moving freestyle, but her event was the
breaststroke. To do the stroke correctly, you must use
your arms to pull forward, skimming the surface of
the water. You then tuck your head down to stream-

line the body for the long push forwards with the whip kick. In this case, Linda's head tuck was right into a floating mass of small, transparent, squishy jellyfish: face first, of course. She remembers that day as the only time she got out of the water and cried.

She had been so distracted by the damned jellyfish that she did not swim very well. The team that was hosting the event was used to such conditions. They kept assuring everyone that the jellyfish were nothing to worry about, explaining that they showed up seasonally and didn't sting. Linda's team did the best they could but complained of the whole affair for months afterwards. She knows many swimmers who are open water swimmers. To accomplish their goals, they have to take into account all the many obstacles and living organisms in natural waters. The jellyfish may not have bothered them.

Every year the Mud Sharks participate in an open water relay event across Lake Tahoe, in the Sierra

Nevada Mountains, on the border of California and Nevada. It is a very deep, very cold lake. Apparently it is one of the highlights of the year for open water swimmers. They usually drive up a few days before the event to acclimate, not only to the water temperature, but also to the diminished oxygen level in the high mountains. Each team of 6 swimmers is accompanied by a motorboat.

No wet suits are allowed. The trick, they say, is to wear an extra-insulated cap, preventing the body's heat from escaping through the exposed head. *That's supposed to make the cold bearable?* Linda's not too sure.

She did have a brief open water adventure with Jodie and Mark one Thanksgiving weekend in California. Jeri was celebrating the holiday on Nantucket Island and happened to mention that she was going to jump into the ocean on Thanksgiving Day, just to say she did it. Always competitive, Jodie, Mark and Linda decided to do the same thing on the West Coast, in Santa Cruz.

In California, the day was sunny, with only a mild cool breeze reminding them that it was winter. They brought Mom along as a witness and got her situated on a bench overlooking the beach. The trio proceeded onto the sand. On the inside, Linda was feeling reluctant and scared to get into the cold water, but anyone watching would have seen a confident swimmer walking straight into the surf. She didn't realize how strong the waves could be as the first one knocked her down and she was immediately submerged up to her shoulders. *Phew! Cold! Invigorating!* The shock of the temperature made her heart rate increase as she tried very hard not to hyperventilate. Mark asked, "Do people have heart attacks doing this?" Apparently the increased heart rate and breathing are normal reactions. *Try to keep moving to get the blood flowing*, she told herself. In a pool, she would start swimming, but she wasn't so sure of any prolonged immersion in this cold water. Linda decided to use a different tactic to keep warm. She ran out of the surf, and back in a few times, only up to her chest.

Then her brother made the announcement that the plunge was not legitimate unless they dove into an oncoming wave. *How bad could that be?* She was already wet and felt pretty good running around in the shallow water. When an appropriate wave started to build and come closer, Linda, Mark and Jodie simultaneously dove in. It was so cold that Linda's head hurt; she then understood the importance of having an insulated cap. That was the end of the adventure. Getting out, they noticed a crowd of on-lookers had gathered, watching to see who was crazy enough to get in the cold water. When they returned to the safety and warmth of her sister's house, it was mentioned that the water temperature of the ocean that day was 56 degrees.

After that experience, she questioned her friend, renowned Open Water swimmer Phyllis Quinn, why she swam in these cold, dangerous and unpredictable events. Phyllis answered humorously, "I'm not good at flip turns." Linda told her friends that the Thanksgiving feast with her family was wonderful, but the highlight of her trip was the brisk swim in the ocean. She even went so far as to say that she now understands the allure of completing a challenging open water swim. It felt so good when it was over!

However, Linda still has not accompanied her teammates for the Tahoe Swim. The swimmers of the relay are submerged in the water for thirty minutes for their first swim, a much more prolonged time period than running in and out of the shallows along the beach, like she did in Santa Cruz. But then the Tahoe relay gets more challenging. If they haven't arrived at their destination, there are additional swims, ten minutes each. *You mean you have to get back in the water?*

Lots of towels, blankets and sleeping bags are onboard the boats to help keep everyone warm between their swims. The water temperature is typically in the high 50s. Her teammates say you get used to it after the initial shock. Apparently the surface is the warmest spot, but when you drop your legs down only a foot or so, well, that's when the cold of the lake really makes itself known. Linda understands the camaraderie that can be built with such an endeavor, but the deep, cold water does not appeal to her. Maybe once, sometime in the future, she'll change her mind and just do it. Maybe.

Almost involuntarily, she breathes more deeply

while initiating the next stroke in this lap and thinks about a very brave lady friend of hers who not only does the Tahoe Swim, but also has swum numerous times under the Golden Gate Bridge, from Baker Beach on the northwest tip of the San Francisco peninsula to the Marin County headlands. Technically speaking, the swim is just outside the Gate, out in the ocean, dealing with the very deep cold water, fast moving tides, large ships, small boats, and yes, jellyfish.

Linda's friend uses three different strokes to accomplish this: the crawl or freestyle, mostly, but when she wanted to make sure she was staying on course, she swam the breaststroke. Linda asked her about swimming under the iconic Golden Gate Bridge and she described how she flipped over to do the backstroke to appreciate the whole view. On one of these swims, her son was waiting for her on the quay at Cavallo Point and chided his mother for taking the risk of swimming

such a dangerous course. One thing must be noted here—this lovely, gutsy lady is twenty years Linda's senior. Linda asked how she could accomplish such a scary and dangerous feat. She responded kindly, "You must conquer your fears, dear."

How did she know that Linda has a fear of anything that could be hiding under the water, like the water moccasins slithering in the lake in Florida. Linda's direct contact with the jellyfish at the meet made the snakes seem unimportant. She would take the presence of a poisonous snake that was trying to avoid her any day over those slimy little buggers. But, comparatively speaking, she'd happily accept some small jellyfish in the water over whatever lurked in the deep water under Lake Tahoe or just outside the Golden Gate. Today Linda appreciates the fact that she can see the bottom and the edges of this pool very clearly, with no monsters hiding in the depths. She makes a two-handed touch and begins another lap.

BREASTSTROKE *LAP SEVEN*

The most important memory she has of
swimming in the UK—drinking beer.

Right now at this meet, Linda is exerting herself to finish these laps as quickly as possible, but in
other situations, breaststroke can be a calming stroke.
It's the stroke one falls back on to relax, look around
and swim leisurely. When Linda swims at her family's cabin in Brant Lake, New York, she often does
the breaststroke. It's almost like floating, yet moving
along ever so slowly. Having her head out of the water
allows her to appreciate the beauty of the lake and the
mountains. Doing the breaststroke also allows Linda
to stay in one place when the current of the lake is attempting to move her down shore a bit, and allows her
to look around to get her bearings.

Swimming was helpful to find her bearings again
when Linda went away for her junior year abroad, in
Merry Olde England. She was in Leeds, 180 miles
north of London. Before she studied there, her only
reference to Leeds had been the 1970 album by The
Who, entitled *Live at Leeds*. She soon learned a lot

about the industrial city in central England. Housed with foreign students, she had the downstairs apartment of a three-story house. Her housemates who lived upstairs were from Scotland and Ireland—you know, the other foreigners.

Although she was there to study her major of mathematics, with a minor in music, one of the first things she did upon arriving was to join the swimming team as a way to meet like-minded friends. At the time, Leeds University did not have their own pool, so the team went to the nearby Carnegie College to use their facilities. The pool was small and old fashioned in style and reminded Linda of the tiled, inner city YWCA pools she swam in as a youngster. It was indoors, 20 yards long, only four lanes, and overly heated. The air was suffused with the strong smell of chlorine. During practices, the water sloshed against the walls adding a large back wash to any movement. Sometimes the turbulence felt like she was trying to swim in a churning washing machine. Modern pools have a grating around the pool which catches the run off as the water crests the edges; this keeps the surface relatively calm. It took Linda a while to get comfortable swimming in such a tiny pool. In retrospect, it provided excellent training.

However, as always with swimming, the benefits outweighed the negatives. Besides helping her to meet new friends with a common interest, the team traveled almost every weekend for competitions. This was a great way to see the rest of the country, swimming all over the UK. The ancient Danish Viking settlement of York was to the east. The famous Beatles town of Liverpool was to the west. She visited Scarborough by the Sea, made famous in the song by Simon and Garfunkel and toured the magnificent Cathedral at Canterbury. Linda's team also traveled north to Newcastle, where Newcastle Ale is brewed, which brings Linda to the most important memory she has of swimming in the UK—drinking beer.

As it turned out, the swimmers on this particular team practiced their sport only as an exercise to spend time in the water and burn calories. They could then, in good conscience, go to the pub and consume mass quantities of English beer. The pub visits seemed to be the main objective. This actually gave Linda an advantage. Again she found herself to be one of the fastest women

on the team. In fact, the other teammates were not too sure of her; she seemed to be a bit "too keen." In other words, she was trying too hard, and they teased her about it all year. Her year in England left Linda with lifelong memories. In fact she could easily lose herself in thought here, and perhaps swim more than the required laps for this race. *Where am I? Wow! Almost done!*

All of this is making Linda think about food. She hadn't eaten much that morning, and now she was well into her race day. She thought about what she could snack on when she got out of the water. She brought a bag of nuts and some protein bars. They'll taste good and give her energy for her next swims. Sharlene recommends liquid hydration, small amounts of protein and some carbohydrates during these competitions. It's too early to have a pint of ale, although that is what she would do, if she were in England.

BREASTSTROKE *LAP EIGHT*

If she can do this grueling event, and everyone
thinks she's smiling, then so much the better.

Linda makes her final two-handed touch, turns and pushes off with only one more lap to go, keeping her head straight and low like she's been taught. In fact, her chin skims so close to the surface of the water when she breathes that she has to open her mouth quite widely to get in as much air as possible. Her facial expression was misconstrued by one of her teammates. They mentioned afterwards that Linda must love the breaststroke; she was smiling throughout her race. If she can do this grueling event, and everyone thinks she's smiling, then so much the better. In reality, it feels more like a grimace and sometimes makes her cheeks ache afterwards. But, at this point in the race she does have something to smile about because she's nearing the end. There's no need for any of her teammates to yell out how many more laps she has to go; she knows very well that this is the last one. Her arms quicken the pace. *Pull, breathe, kick.*

She can hear cheering. Yelling and cheering are

common sounds at a swimming meet, but the crowd seems extra loud. *It must be a close race.* She's taking some seconds to look around now to see what's going on. She doesn't usually do that. It's difficult to move her head sideways, so usually she's only catching glimpses of those up ahead of her. Her teammate Greg is a champion in the breaststroke. His head is always darting from side to side, keeping an eye on the other competitors. Perhaps that motivates him to swim so fast.

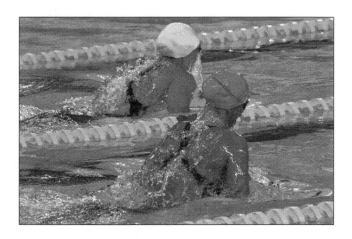

As she tilts her head slightly, she can see that there's a swimmer in the next lane moving right along with her. She realizes now that the cheering is for them. Linda is the one in the very close race and she's sprinting as fast as she can! One swimmer is already finished, so this is not a fight for the win, but a close race, nevertheless, is still exciting. This is the best part of this sport and Linda would love to be in the stands cheering, appreciating the efforts, if she weren't the one in the water right now.

When Linda saw televised results of past Olympics, she noticed that the attention, the cheering and the cameras were focused only on the winners. She felt sympathy for the others who finished behind the frontrunners. Their names aren't mentioned, and the cameras leave them behind. They too had made it to the Olympics and were among the best in the world. Second and third runner-up finishes can be just as exciting.

Now she's sprinting as fast as she can, breathing hard. The black T comes into view. Gulping air, she asks her legs to do one last hard kick, and finally, finally she makes it to the wall. Her two handed touch is almost an assault. She hits the pad as hard as she can to ensure contact with the electronics, as a huge sigh of relief involuntarily leaves her body. Linda glanced up at the scoreboard; she had swum the eight laps quickly, posting a fast, personal best, 3:46.02. The woman in the next lane, Cindy Myer, had come in closely behind with a 3:46.17. Linda reaches over and shakes her hand. It was a good race, and she knew that the extra push by Cindy helped her do so well.

She can't believe how tired she is. All her daydreaming had occupied her mind, so she didn't feel the exertion until she finished. Maybe that was a good thing. Anyway, she's very relieved her hardest events are over. Linda climbs out of the pool and proceeds to the warm up pool to do some leisurely breaststroke, look around, and catch her breath. After a few laps, her breathing starts to slow and return to normal. Sharlene comes to the edge of the warm-up pool. Laughing, she hopes Linda will also be amused. Turns out Linda placed 11th in her 200 breaststroke and her next lane rival Cindy placed 12th. *You have to be kidding me,* thought Linda, *another 11th place, in the Nationals, just out of range for a medal, again!* She had swum well, posted a good time, but 11th place?

These repeated eleventh place finishes were getting to be a joke back at the tent where Linda's team was resting. She accepted all the good-natured joshing from her teammates, having to admit that there was a comical aspect to it all.

TEN

4x50 FREESTYLE RELAY

"Don't forget the relays. We needed you for those..."

Competitive swimming is considered an individual sport, judged by accumulated individual points and records, except for the relays—four individuals work together for a single purpose: the fastest finish. The shared responsibility builds connections that last and make relays fun. In fact, some Masters swimmers come to the meets only to swim in relays.

Most of the medals Linda received in her early years of swimming had come from her participation in relays. In other words, her successes were only from team efforts; she did not have many individual triumphs. In a fit of self pity, she once told her mom that she didn't want to save any of these medals because none of them were won by her alone. Her mother kindly reminded her that those medals could not have been won without her participation. Linda had indeed done her part and earned those medals; she didn't let the team down! They reside in her house, in the bottom of a trunk... somewhere.

As an adult, swimming on relays helped Linda feel important and relevant to her team. She was embarrassed at a meet where she only placed in one event, fifth place, at that. She earned a measly 4 points for the whole day. She lamented to her coach's husband that she added only 4 points. He kindly responded that each point counts, adding. "Don't forget the relays. We needed you for those. You swam well and didn't let the team down." That consoling statement embodies the philosophy of US Masters Swimming: welcoming and accepting of everyone, with a special respect for all who "have what it takes" to be a competitive swimmer at any level of skill.

His comment reminded Linda of a particular 4X100 mens' freestyle relay from a few years back. The event was starting and Coach could only find three of the swimmers. Everyone was asking where the fourth man was. The announcer's voice came over the loudspeaker repeatedly calling out the name of the missing member of the relay. Other teammates frantically checked the bathrooms and all around the pool, with no luck. The electronic buzzer sounded and the relays began. The first swimmer swam his four laps. The second swimmer went off the blocks, and still no fourth man. This was so nerve-wracking for the whole team. The third man swam, and there was nobody there to swim the last leg of the race. They were disqualified. *I will never forget that upsetting moment!*

All the other competing teams continued on. The

usual spirited yelling and cheering around the pool was deafening, but the noise coming from Linda's area had stopped; nothing but eerie silence. Relays constitute a big part of the team points and that particular relay had a good chance of coming in first. They had lost a big one.

Half an hour later, the missing man casually walked up to the team's tented area. "Oh," he said casually, "I must have missed the relay." He had been out in his car listening to music as a way of relaxing before his event. He apologized to Coach and the team, especially to those who had exerted themselves for nothing. It was disappointing, but the show must go on. Despite the setback, her team did quite well at that particular meet, coming in first in their division. That event answered Linda's nagging thought that swimming on a relay does not add to an individual's accomplishments. She now knows that each leg of the relay is important; the group is only strong if everyone strives to do their best. No one wants to be the weak link.

One of Linda's best memories involves an unusual relay. She registered for a local meet because it offered a 100-yard relay, each swimmer swimming only one lap. The 100-yard relay is not officially listed for USMS swimming, so this one was scheduled just for fun.

When Linda arrived at the meet, she discovered that only one other teammate had signed up. You can't have a relay with only two participants. Coach Sharlene was determined to remedy the problem. The event was not sanctioned and did not count for any points, so the make-up of the relays could be unconventional, mixed up with swimmers from different teams. She searched the pool area for two volunteers to help the Mud Sharks fill out a relay card. Linda talks a lot about Laura Val, the World Record Holder. As it turned out that day, Laura and her equally accomplished teammate Rich Burns were the only two representing their team, the Tamalpais Aquatic Masters. Both agreed to the "just for fun" relay.

Laura dove in and very quickly swam 25-yards. Linda's teammate Greg was next, from the far end, racing towards Linda who was on the blocks, breathing deeply, readying for heavy exertion. A smile crossed her face as she noticed Greg didn't "look around" during this sprint. He swam so fast, it was over before he had time to check out his competition. *Here he comes.*

There's the touch. Off the blocks I go! She swam her best and made a solid touch at the far wall. One lap and done. *That was fun!* After Rich sped through his lap, the race was over.

Linda was the slowest of the four, in other words, the weak link, but in this instance it didn't matter. She could not stop smiling; she had swum on a relay with Laura Val. What a proud moment!

She remembers watching an amazing swim at the 2008 Beijing Olympics: the finals of the Men's 4X100 Freestyle Relay. In that particular race, France was favored. Olympian Rowdy Gaines was on hand offering commentary. He mentioned that however the numbers were combined, it looked like France had a faster relay team; the United States was slated to come in second.

Michael Phelps made history at the Beijing Olympics winning ten gold medals, and this relay played a major part in that accomplishment. He led off for the first leg impressively swimming 100 meters, Garrett Weber-Gale, in his first Olympic appearance sped down the pool, flipped and came charging back. Cullen Jones listed third, sprinted all out and finished behind the French by .059 seconds. Jason Lezak, in an historic, amazing, some say epic swim, not only caught up with the French champion Alain Bernard, but out-touched him by .08 of a second. Jason swam the 100-meter freestyle in 46.06 seconds, eclipsing the then world record by more than a second. Astoundingly fast. Linda has watched the video of that swim over and over and still gets a thrill.

~~~~~~

And now it's her turn: the relays are about to start. Sharlene makes the rounds, gathering all participants, letting everyone know what heat they're in, what lane number, and in what order each will swim. She's calling for James, Don, Linda and the newest member of the Mud Sharks, Linda's sister, Jeri. The Mud Sharks are accustomed to this routine of relay preparation, but having Linda's sister there made it special. They all hear the call, grab their caps and goggles, and proceed to the pool deck.

It was winning a relay that brought fame to the Hepworth family in the summer of 1968. And it was the chance for the sisters to revive that relay in 2009 that brought Linda back into the world of competitive swimming. Today, with just two sisters present, there wasn't the same exhilaration that came with everyone together, but it was still something special, another family relay at a Championship meet. When the sisters were focused on these swims, it made them forget the small squabbles about who had not done their chores, or which sister had borrowed someone else's favorite jeans the week before.

This event is the Mixed (both men and women) 4X50 Freestyle Relay. Don and James are two very fast swimmers from Linda's team. Adding up their times, Linda's coach said they had a good chance of winning a medal, compared to the previous year's final results. There's a festive feeling as the relay swimmers from all the teams begin to congregate. Linda and her teammates stick together in the crowd and maneuver to get in line behind the starting block of their designated lane.

A long whistle sounds. James steps up onto the starting block. He'll be first, leading the team today. "Take your mark." James crouches and with the sound of the electronic buzzer, he's off the blocks, streaming through the water for two laps of freestyle. Looking good, he's holding his own against the other swimmers. He makes a solid flip turn and heads back on his second lap.

Don stands on the blocks, arms outstretched, in anticipation of his start. He's got his eyes on James who is now kicking home strongly, arms churning. Don waits for James to "attack the wall" with a punch for a finish. This is important in a relay because the next swimmer is sometimes barely hanging on, already in motion, anticipating that decisive touch.

Don is in the water. Once a relay starts, it goes very quickly. Linda watches his familiar powerful stroke. She and Don have been swimming together at practices for more than five years. She sees him do his unique freestyle turn and start swimming back towards her. The coach had the two fast men go first to "frontload" the relay, in other words, give the sisters an extra lead.

It's Linda's turn. She takes a deep breath and steps up onto the slanted starting block. She plants one foot forward, and bends her knees. Her arms are outstretched and her hands are following Don in as he finishes his lap. *There it is... the touch*, and off she goes.

The water feels cool, only momentarily, as she enters and begins her strokes. *Kick hard*, she says to herself. This is a fifty, only two laps. She can see her arms, reaching, pulling through one by one. She's back to her familiar freestyle. *Breathe regularly, set your pace.* She's almost at the far wall. *Pull, pull, kick, kick. Deep breath, somersault, push-off; it's all happening so fast!*

Excellent! She timed that right and made a good turn with a solid footing. This flip turn is so important: there's only one. Losing time on a botched turn is not something she wants to do. There's more at stake here because she's part of a team, and she doesn't want to let anyone down. She's on her last lap. *Bring it home, Linda. Give it your all!* Her arms are a blur and all she can hear is the sound of water splashing and her own hard breathing as she gulps as much air as she can with each breath. The black line seems like it's going on forever. *Sometimes one lap feels like an eternity! Stroke, stroke…there are the flags,* finally, her friends, the welcoming backstroke flags. Three more strokes, the T-bar, and the definitive connection to the wall. She senses the splash of Jeri diving over her, swimming the last leg, the anchor leg.

Linda stays in the water, recovering from her exertion. It's all she can do to hang onto the lane lines, catch her breath, and stay out of the way. She has company. Both James and Don are "hanging out" in the lane waiting for everyone to finish. Jeri is returning strongly, her last lap of the day. Looking fast and competent, she's really moving right along. Linda is impressed; she knows Jeri is not usually a sprinter. A strong finish, a hard definitive touch and it's all over again, in a little more than 2 minutes.

The sisters have done it again—adding another event to their family's swimming history. Earlier Linda heard the coach say that the "field was deep" at this competition today. There were 29 teams swimming in the 55+ age group, determined by the youngest swimmer on the relay. The Mud Shark's 4X50 Freestyle Relay placed 16th. Not in the Top 10 for a medal as they had hoped, but not a bad showing at all. As a unit, the four teammates walk to the warm-down pool for a few leisurely laps. Staying together, they head back to the tent to rest up.

In 2010, Linda swam the backstroke on a 200-Meter Medley Relay along with her amazing Mud Sharks teammates: Eric, Don and Gillian. They placed first! To add to the victory, their time was recorded as one of the top ten in the world that year! Linda did not hesitate to send off for her patch to commemorate the event. She wears that Top 10 patch proudly on the sleeve of her team coat, even though it's "only for a relay."

Linda has one more event to go.

ELEVEN

THE FINAL RACE

Gone is the anxiety that had plagued her this morning.
The refreshingly cool water revives her.

A long shadow encroaches over the pool, pushing the bright sunlight away, marking the hours as they pass. It has been a long day for both the swimmers and the officials. Many months before, when she was registering and selecting her events for this meet, she was pleased to see that she could end the day with a relatively easy race for her-fifty yards of backstroke.

Linda had been feeling noticeably tired from swimming the 500 early that morning, two additional long events and the relay with her sister, but jumping into the water for the fifth time that day feels wonderful. Gone is the anxiety that had plagued her this morning. The refreshingly cool water revives her. Feeling strong, she thinks, *I can do this, only two laps of the pool, on my back, face up.* Laughingly she tells herself that she might even look around to enjoy the trip down and back.

"Take your mark." Linda plants her feet on the wall and pulls her torso up, head back. With the whistle, she's off. Her arms know what to do and her legs join in with a strong kick. *Breathe, swing your arms up, pull down strongly, breathe, repeat…*

Eighteen strokes later she's at the far wall. She turns over onto her stomach, makes her half somersault and pushes off. Swimming her last lap of the day, there's no looking around, no daydreaming; just the intent to backstroke her way home as quickly as she can. This one is over fast. She swims her 50 in a good time: 39.65 seconds, smiles as she finishes and heads to the warm-down pool for the last plunge of the day.

~~~

And what a leisurely swim it is. She does breaststroke, a bit of backstroke and some freestyle, all very relaxed, completely enjoying the water. Gone is the stress of the competitions behind her. She has finished for the day; her races are done. As her mind begins yet another dreamy reverie, a familiar voice brings her back to the present. It's Jeri, very excitedly gesturing on the edge of the pool with some welcome news, saying something about a medal. The results are in for this last race, her 50-yard back-stroke. Linda had come in 10th and won a medal! Finally, a medal!

No more humility for Linda. No more quiet acceptance that 11th place is good enough. She checked the posted results again and sure enough it was true. She had won a medal and it made all the difference. As she headed to the awards table, the last event of the day, the Mens 50-yard backstroke, was in the water. When the last heat finished, the whistles and electronic buzzers that had been so constant during the day went silent. The meet was over.

TWELVE

This competition is over; preparation for the next one begins.

As she showers and dresses in the locker room, Linda relishes all the conversations amongst the other competitors. Most of the talk concerns the next competition, when and where they will all see each other and do this again. The next pressing issue, dinner plans with the family. Everyone is exhausted, exhilarated and ravenously hungry. Linda steps outside to the pool again for the final time of the day to join her family, wearing her team jacket with her shiny medal on its

colorful ribbon prominently displayed. Sharlene is there saying goodbye, complimenting all her swimmers for what a great job they did, adding a reminder to be back at the pool tomorrow! This competition is over; preparation for the next one begins.

Leaving the aquatic complex, Linda looks back at the pools. The bleachers are empty. Gone is the sea of canopies and tents that covered the officials and housed the teams. All the participants are leaving and going their separate ways. Workers are dismantling the starting blocks and rolling up the lane lines. This time, there is no sadness at leaving the water behind. It's been a great day with short bursts of heavy exertion generously interspersed with restful memories.

At the restaurant, everyone's attention turns to Mom. Literally, none of this would be possible without her. They thank her for being brave enough to

bring five children into the world and give them such grand opportunities. As dinner is served a quiet settles over the table. It is enough to eat dinner, smile, and appreciate all their accomplishments as a family. Everyone is tired after such a long day. The goodbyes are accompanied by kisses and lots of hugs. Everyone knows they'll be on the phone together in a few days, planning their next adventure.

As this memorable day comes to an end, Linda is at home resting, her mind filled with images of the day. The memory of her arms swinging over her head, with their metered backstroke rhythm, provide a shutter dividing the scenes passing before her eyes: her mother and family cheering her on, her sister Jeri's smile as they finish their 500, her hands making a solid two-handed touch to finish her challenging breaststroke race. She's reliving her relief upon seeing the backstroke flags finally coming into view as she was completing her last lap. She can't help but grin as she recalls the moment she read on the results sheet, "50-Yard Backstroke: 10th Place, Linda Hepworth," finally earning her medal. She will hold it again tomorrow, straighten out the ribbon, and show it to all her friends.

It's quiet in her room now, but she still hears heartfelt cheering and splashing water sounds, and sees swimmers racing past, with the bright light of the afternoon sun dancing on the surface of the water. It was such a special, wonderful day filled with heartfelt challenges and awesome inspiration. Swimming has brought that to her life, and she can't wait to do it all over again.

THIRTEEN

The turtle is still going strong.

Recently, Linda ran into a woman who knew the Hepworth family's swimming history. This lady, not meaning to offend, asked Linda how she felt about the fact that all her sisters could beat her. Although the comment stung, it was the truth.

Soon after that meeting, she found some old newspaper clippings. One from 1972 caught Linda's attention. Her sister Tracy is pictured on the left with friend and teammate Patrice Maloney after winning first and

second places at the Nationals in the grueling 400 IM. Patrice clocked an incredible time of 5:14.5 and Tracy came in second with a time of 5:16.8. Tracy had won another gold medal for her partcipation in the 800-freestyle relay, with a time of 8:45.0 — a full four seconds ahead of the second place team.

Later in the article, Both Jodie and Linda are mentioned for their performances in the 500 freestyle. Jodie placed 7th with 6:03.9 and Linda came in 12th with a time of 6:16.9. So, the USMS Nationals in 2014 was not the first time Linda had swum a 500 free! She had apparently completed the event in 1972, with her youngest sister beating her by 13 seconds - an eternity in swimming terms. No wonder she had forgotten about it!

The Middies are mentioned as being the winning team at the two previous Nationals, in Toledo, Ohio in 1970 and in Springfield, Ill. in 1971: truly a championship team, with many fast swimmers competing. Linda swam along, but was never in the top tier.

Resuming her swimming career, those memories remained in the back of her thoughts. She was bolstered by a comment made by Julia, one of her Mud Sharks teammates, "It's not how fast you swim, but how you look up on the blocks." Taking that to heart and to compensate for not winning, Linda usually wears a colorful bathing suit! Winning the 10th place medal at the Nationals changed everything; all the nagging doubts about her abilities disappeared.

Now she is happy, and still slightly surprised, that she is faring well against other swimmers her age. She earned four Top 10 medals at the Summer National Championships, held in Gresham, Oregon in 2016. Recently she won three 1st place ribbons and three 2nd place ribbons at the Pacific Masters Long Course Championships in 2018. After all this time, Linda can still swim, and swim well. The turtle is still going, even though the hares, at one time, may have been faster.

FOURTEEN

Dreamy water thoughts

Water has been a prevalent element in Linda's life. Most of her memories are of clean, safe waters for swimming, for drinking and bathing, for life. But she knows that it also has a dark side, a destructive side. Twice she was surrounded by such waters: a hurricane in Florida and a flood in Northern California.

She was a young girl when the hurricane came through. Linda, her sisters and brother were naively celebrating the storm. There was no school for a few days and their mother had stocked the pantry in case there was a washout. Those were the important things: no school and lots to eat! They were too young to consider the dangerous facts that their house could lose its roof or be completely blown away.

As the wind was howling, Linda's mother told the kids that there was going to be a quiet time, the eye of the storm, and it meant that the storm was half over. After a few hours of torrential rain and winds, there was a beautiful calm. The eye had its own magnetic anomaly going on, with a unique stillness in the air, making the colors of the lake, the lawn and the sky very crisp and radiant. Linda wanted to run outside but wisely did not. She kept watch from the safety of her room as the sky then darkened, and the second wave of the hurricane passed, thankfully leaving their home intact. The storm mixed beauty and strength.

The second big water event in her life happened when she was awakened by someone yelling to get a pump going. *A pump*, she questioned, as the word reverberated through her thoughts. *Why would someone be yelling for a pump at 7:00 in the morning?* Slowly, the commotion started to make sense. It had been raining heavily for days and there had been a public notice on the TV the previous evening to watch for high tides. She was up and moving when she realized that a small arm of San Francisco Bay, Las Gallinas Creek, had overflowed its banks and was encroaching up her street, flooding the lower level homes.

That water was strong, but certainly not beautiful. It was muddy, salty, cold and very scary. When water is on the move like that, it sweeps up everything in its path. Linda's house was a bit higher than some and was thankfully saved from the onslaught of the unwanted waters.

Sometimes the problem is not too much water, but not enough. Linda has lived through several severe droughts, with rainstorms coming only intermittently. She now celebrates each drop that falls from the sky and does not understand why the weather reports forecast gloom and despair whenever the much-needed rain is predicted. Maybe it's because rainy days are usually associated with sadness, especially in music. Without them there would be no raindrops falling on Burt Bacharach's head. There would be no rhythm of the falling rain for the Cascades to melodically describe a feeling of loss. The band Flash and the Pan would have had to use something else to portray the dark mood described in *Walking, Walking in the Rain.*

Linda delights in warm summer rains in New York and light refreshing showers in Florida that cut through the heavy damp air. She knows the beauty of prismatic raindrops left on leaves and the glistening of wet sidewalks reflecting the moonlight. In the more arid western United States rain refreshes the air, brings life to the desert and fills the rushing rivers for the trout and salmon.

Linda spent a year in England's famous damp climate and not only thrived, but returned home with a rosy complexion commonly said to be a result of the English rain. Linda's neighbors know her to take long walks in the rain, bundled up with boots and an umbrella. She can go on and on about the pleasures of rain, of baths, and of swimming.

Tomorrow she'll unwind with a walk on her favorite beach. A stroll along the water's edge, listening to the rhythmic crashing of the surf is just what she needs to refresh her mind and her body. The ocean waters soothe her. Shimmering mountain lakes entice her. The gentle rain sings to her and clear swimming pools invite her. It's the water that brings her comfort. The water beckons.

ACKNOWLEDGMENTS

I want to thank everyone who so lovingly helped me with this book. My family is first on the list. Thank you all for allowing me to write about our lives, both public and private, for supporting me in the water as well as on dry land, reading, re-reading and editing my numerous manuscripts, and giving me new insights.

I heartily thank Petie Connolly for her help in the 500 Freestyle and Dr. Stephanie Blackton for her unwavering friendship through the decades. Coaches Jackie White (grade school), Warren Beaulieu (high school), and Shirley Carmichael (college), patiently taught me the basics of swimming and competition.

I thank United States Masters Swimming and Pacific Masters Swimming Associations. Everyone has been so welcoming and supportive. It is not easy putting together these competitions, maintaining the integrity of the sport, keeping records, and providing adults a place to swim, recreate and stay in shape. I am proud to be a member.

The Rolling Hills Mud Sharks! Coach Sharlene Van Boer! Thank you for inviting me to be a Mud Shark. As Sharlene says, "We are not only a team, we are a family." The affectionate, enthusiastic cheering coming from the Mud Sharks at any event, attests to that sentiment. "Go Mud Sharks!"

I posthumously thank Angar Mora. He spent his life in search of art, light and beauty in this world and dubbed me a Weaver of Memories. He understood. May he rest in peace.

I especially thank my editor, Carol Callahan. She has expertly and patiently guided me through every phase of the publishing of my three books: *If These Tables Could Talk*, 2010; *Turning the Tables*, 2012; and now *The Water Beckons*, 2019. She, along with Sherry Issa, suggested the subject of my third book. "People are interested in what we used to do when we were young. You should write about how you got back into swimming." *The Water Beckons* is that story.

Thank you all.

Made in the USA
San Bernardino, CA
28 May 2019